ARAPAWA —
ONCE UPON AN ISLAND

ARAPAWA —
ONCE UPON AN ISLAND

BETTY ROWE

The
Halcyon
Press

Published by

The Halcyon Press

A division of

Halcyon Publishing Ltd.

C.P.O. Box 360, Auckland, New Zealand.

Printed by

Colorcraft Ltd

Hong Kong

Typeset by
Glenfield Graphics Ltd
Finished Art by
Michelle Tack

ISBN 0 908685 21 1

Copyright ® 1988 Betty Rowe.

Contents

Dedicated to:

The wildlife of Arapawa,
especially, Sam and Jody

Acknowledgments

My sincere thanks to all who contributed to the saga of the Arapawa wildlife and made the story unfold for the telling.

Grateful thanks to Mr A. R. Werner of England for his great assistance and continuing interest. His endeavours on behalf of the goats have been extremely important in helping to establish the credentials of the Arapawa goat.

A special thanks to Mr Max Rogers for his encouragement and faith in the manuscript, his willingness to assist and advise and for his wonderful optimism.

CHAPTER I

The Expatriates

The children lay sleeping in the back of the station wagon and Walt, my husband, was concentrating on the flow of traffic that always plagued our weekend trips to our summer home on the New Jersey coastline. I sat deep in thought, grimacing at the jolting of the car as we inched our way towards the bridge leading to Pennsylvania. Horns blared in protest at the delay and the chemical plant nearby belched nauseous fumes across the congested tangle of cars.

Suddenly the thoughts that had been growing in my mind for many months burst forth. 'Let's chuck it, Walt,' I said with a voice not my own.

'Chuck what, Betty?' came his absent-minded reply as he leaned out the window to assess our progress.

'This life we're leading!' I blurted out. 'There must be a better way, something more to offer the children, something less materialistic, challenge and reality — they're what we need!'

At that moment the reality of the traffic and the challenge of getting to Pennsylvania before midnight were all the problems Walt needed and he didn't bother to answer.

Horns, accompanied by some very descriptive swearing from behind, urged me on. 'We need to get out of this rat race. Let's get away from it all. Go homesteading, wash our clothes in a stream. We could grow our own food and drink goats' milk. Others have done it, why can't we?'

There, I'd said it and, to add defiance to insanity, I leaned out the window and bellowed into the night: 'Stop blowing those horns, you'll wake the kids!'

Obviously, no-one heard, for the din increased with the approaches to various turn-offs, motors gunned in anticipation, ulcers and hypertension working overtime.

Walt remained silent and tight-lipped, which meant one of two things; either he was digesting what I had said or had figured it was my 'time of the month'.

Finally, we crossed the Delaware into Pennsylvania, moving freely at last in the direction of Richboro where we lived. To my surprise,

Walt picked up the threads of my outburst and from what I could make out, agreed with me, although he was quick to point out how improbable it was to even contemplate leaving. We had close family ties, a secure life, made so by a lucrative income that provided for us handsomely, a home we had worked so hard to create. What more, he questioned, did I want?

Desperately searching for words to translate my thoughts into something comprehensible, I blurted; 'I'm sick of P.T.A., Cub Scouts and choir practice. I need clean air and seclusion, but most of all I want to show the children something of life that isn't plastic-wrapped, pre-packaged or garishly advertised on television as a prerequisite to happiness.'

Walt looked at me over his glasses, trying to decipher that somewhat eloquent mouthful and, I imagined, trying to picture me trading in my automatic washing machine and dryer for an icy stream and some bushes. I couldn't quite picture it either and had to admit we'd have a hard time convincing anyone, including ourselves, that money wasn't everything and we'd be a lot better off struggling to survive.

Next morning, the children looked at me over their cornflakes as I enthusiastically painted a picture of the five of us alone on a golden, sunkissed shore — far from pollution, Vietnam, nuclear war and television, lumping them together as some ominous collective threat to their well-being. They all agreed it was as good an idea as any I'd had over the years, but they preferred to stay and take their chances and, grabbing school books and lunch boxes, they ran down the road to the school bus before I could plead my case further.

Walt left late that morning, staying, not to try to divert with friendly persuasion my fixation with swaying palms and icy streams, but rather to reinforce it!

Usually Walt mulls things over for what seems to me an unnecessary length of time before coming to a decision, whereas I jump in boots and all with lightning, if not always accurate, assessments. On this occasion, however, I sensed something different, for Walt seemed as bent on lunacy as I was and it dawned on me that he had been thinking his secret Walter Mitty thoughts too.

But we soon came to realise that there were so many considerations, and at first each of them seemed enough to halt any further thought on the matter.

For 22 years Walt had been a manufacturer's representative and had earned the respect of clients and competitors alike. He owed allegiance to the company which had treated him so fairly and kindly. His fledgling career in the world of business had been broken by a letter from the U.S. Government calling him into the army during the Korean War. This came shortly after our marriage and we had to abandon plans for renovating an old barn that was to have been our first home.

Walt had spent most of his army days jumping from towers of various heights in an effort to become a paratrooper and failed the final test, much to my relief, for had he passed, he would have graduated to the real thing and I was not overjoyed at the prospect of his jumping into space from the military version of a DC3.

He had not gone to Korea because of an over-active thyroid which had caused his eyes to bulge and his nerves to jangle and led to an alarming loss of weight from his 1.8 metre frame. In addition he had contracted a serious case of pneumonia and when he had finally recovered from these ailments (and with two-thirds of his thyroid removed in Fort Benning's army hospital), he hadn't had the required amount of time left to be placed on overseas duty. After the army stint we had returned to Pennsylvania, Walt had taken up his career and we hoped we would learn of war no more.

Mitch arrived in 1954, long, lanky and with wisps of ginger-coloured hair. Two years later, we adopted Mary, just nine months younger than Mitch. A year later, we adopted five-week-old Roy and found ourselves with a household of little people who kept us busy 24 hours a day.

Mitch was quiet and introspective, studious and self-assured. Mary came to us shy and unsure, with luminous dark eyes too old for her years. Roy, by contrast, was a bundle of non-stop energy that had his days and nights mixed up for the first seven months of his life and, during his toddler years, he had more excursions to the family doctor for repairs than Mitch and Mary put together.

The additions to the family meant more room was needed in the inn, and we decided to build our dream house, complete with playroom, den, four bedrooms and downstairs bath. It was a lovely home, deep within two acres of woodland, filled with bird life and bustling with cheeky little gray squirrels. Over the years we raised five of these delightfully naughty creatures that had escaped or fallen from their nests and were found by the children. We also raised a racoon, christened 'Jesse' after the notorious Jesse James and so named because of the facial markings which resembled the mask of a western desperado. Jesse slept with Mary, curled about her head in a live version of Davy Crockett's coon skin cap. Roy slept with a noisy beagle called Pepper and Mitch curled up with one of our several cats or an orphaned baby squirrel.

When school finished on Fridays, we collected the children and animals and headed for our summer home on the Atlantic coast. One of the treats for the children was a stop for an ice-cream cone along the way. Mary had graduated to a double-decker since she obligingly shared hers with the beagle, but after Jesse came on the scene, we found it necessary to increase this to a triple-decker for Mary to have any at all.

Jesse was diapered before our departure and lay on the shelf along the rear window drinking milk from a baby bottle and cars with wide-eyed occupants followed us for miles. If not perched on his window seat, Jesse sat on my shoulder and it was great fun to watch the expressions on the faces of people in passing cars as Jesse peered out unblinkingly, unimpressed by all the attention.

It was a good life. We were blessed with loving parents and large family gatherings where holidays became joyous and fulfilling events. Christmas was a time of bells and carols, secrets and snow, of mistletoe and hidden presents.

Fires blazed brightly on winter nights and, after a day of ice skating or sledding, there were hot chocolate and toasted marshmallows as frozen toes thawed before the fire, and sleepy children nodded in the warm glow until carried to their beds by strong, reassuring arms.

We had friendships, close and warm, and a rich social life full of fun, with pleasant trips to New York for shows and plays. But there were clouds on the horizon, gathering storms of doubt, fear and anxiety. These were the symptoms of Vietnamosis that produced the anxiety that my sons would die, blown to fragments in some faraway jungle for a cause that I did not understand.

John Kennedy was assassinated and the country was plunged into despair and pathos. We mourned and recovered, only to watch on the television screen as Robert Kennedy lay in a pool of blood, his life ebbing away. Martin Luther King was killed for a cause as old as history — the freedom of the oppressed. Kent State students lay dying and city after city burst into flames as the waves of riots swept across the country. I was sickened to see a Vietnamese soldier shot to death before my eyes, his hands tied behind his back. He had not even had a trial. The horror of the Mai L'ai massacre made me recoil with the knowledge that I was somehow involved and responsible. Yellow rain fell on all, friend and foe alike. Children of the enemy screamed in agony as napalm turned them into living balls of fire.

We witnessed the consuming grief of friends whose son was returned in a welded coffin and the unleashed anger of his widow as she refused the flag at his funeral. Friends labelled us as communist sympathisers because of my anti-Vietnam persuasions; others said we would be running away. But, in the end, after many hours of discussion, we decided to make our dream a reality.

How do you explain to family and friends who suddenly find their sustaining love and kinship cast aside with what must have seemed callous disregard? We loved them as much as ever but there was something else, a restlessness within us which we couldn't possibly communicate to them. It left those around us with a sense of rejection and abandonment. Our declarations of 'getting away from it all' brought understanding from a few but for most, it meant we were really getting away from them. We had not been forced to leave but had willingly chosen this course and were walking away from all we professed to hold dear. We were assailed by doubt and remorse about the hurt we caused and our unease was transmitted to the children as they awaited the next turn of events.

'Why New Zealand?' we were asked on many occasions. Why, indeed. I think the stranger who joined me on the beach one afternoon is the man who chartered our course. Our first thoughts had been of Canada, then Australia, but both, after investigation, seemed very like the America we were leaving. The man who sat beside me on the beach had heard of our plans from a neighbour and questioned me as to what we hoped to achieve and where we were heading. I blurted out the now well-rehearsed arguments about clean air, open spaces, home-grown food, challenge and reality, something about realising our full potential under the grand design of self-sufficiency. 'New Zealand,' he said emphatically. 'New Zealand is where you want to go.'

My unnamed counsellor knew the country intimately and assured me that all we were searching for could be found in this underpopulated, unpolluted, windswept paradise. It was this chance conversation that led us to the New Zealand Embassy in Washington D.C. where we were promptly told we didn't stand a chance of immigrating!

The reasons given were our ages (we were then nearly 40) and the fact that Walt was not a trained craftsman and had no job to go to. Our only hope lay in having enough money to see us through. We could do little about the ageing process but we set about rectifying the monetary requirement in an effort to present ourselves as worthy of acceptance.

We sold all our lifetime's possessions, eyeing each item with the hard, cold appraisal of the prospective buyer. One by one, the familiar things that made up our home were sold, their comforting presence exchanged for dollars in the bank. The children watched with uncomprehending eyes as their toys and furniture were carted away and we added up the growing column of figures that replaced all we treasured.

Not soon enough, or too soon (I was never sure) the day of the final goodbyes arrived. Clutching passports, tickets and bank book, our bridge to the Antipodes, we entered Philadelphia International Airport accompanied by a retinue of sombre friends and crying relatives. The farewells had been going on for the previous three months but this was the real thing. Suddenly we realised we would never again see some of those beloved people who stood there that day.

It is difficult to describe the feeling that enveloped us. We were full of excitement and anticipation at the adventure ahead, yet at the same moment there was an irresistible urge to have the clock stand still, to keep the familiar faces in focus and the sights and sounds of our homeland around us.

Amidst good wishes and pronouncements that we would be back in six months, recovered from our folly and restored to our senses, we slowly made our way to the turnstile. Tears rolled down our faces and those of the people who came to say goodbye as we raised a parting toast to one another with the champagne our friends had brought for the occasion. We waved until we were airborne and the door to yesterday closed forever.

We flew over the chequered fields, mountains and finally the Pacific coast. There we bade our silent, final farewells to Americana and all we had ever known. Hawaii, Samoa and the last lap to New Zealand; the hours filled with excited chatter as we strained to get a glimpse through the clouds of our newly adopted country.

Our first impressions were of rolling hills, neatly fenced paddocks and millions upon millions of sheep. People were generally friendly and warm, many inviting us into their homes, obviously wanting to talk about life in America, while we tried politely to steer the conversation to life in New Zealand.

We decided to start at the very top and booked a tour of Northland with Cape Reinga as the first stop. We climbed gigantic dunes and basked in the marvellous scenery, marvelling at Ninety Mile Beach, which in the States would have long ago been laid waste by the developer — another Miami or Malibu.

In Kaitaia, we temporarily misplaced Roy and had the hotel in an uproar with guests, waitresses, housemaids and the manager joining the search. Mitch looked in the men's rooms and showers while Walt, Mary and I roamed the hotel halls and lobby. He was nowhere to be found. More than a little concerned, I headed back to the room to see if he had turned up and turning a corner, collided with my half-naked child, towel about his midriff, dripping his way to our rooms!

'Roy!' I exclaimed, hugging him in relief. 'Where have you been — we've searched everywhere for you?'

'I was having a bath.'

We explained that Mitch had made a thorough search of the men's facilities. So just where had he soaked?

'In the Laddies' Room!'

'In the what?' And guiding us down the corridor, he pointed to the unoccupied Ladies' Room!

Everyone had been calling the boys 'lads' since our arrival. Roy had seen the sign and managed to go undetected into the women's ablution block. Had one of the female guests decided to bathe, her shrieks might have helped us to find him, as the presence of a strapping twelve-year-old was not likely to be welcomed. As it was, I made a mental note to give Roy a refresher course in spelling.

We drew further attention to ourselves at breakfast. Sitting down amidst curious stares from guests and staff, we found ourselves facing an amazing array of cutlery. Knives, forks and spoons of varying sizes surrounded each plate and we felt all eyes upon us as we proceeded to use all the inappropriate ones for the several courses, the kitchen staff peering at us through a crack in the door.

We were relieved when the table was cleared and the waitress brought us tea. I handed one teapot to Walt and poured from the other, only to find it contained hot water!

'Walt,' I whispered. 'They forgot the tea in this one!'

A sympathetic guest saved us further embarrassment by leaning over his table and whispering that the tea came in one pot and the hot water for diluting in another. Then, placing his napkin to his lips to hide his smile, he swivelled around and resumed his breakfast.

After two weeks of indulgent sightseeing, we began to look seriously for employment. The North Island offered us everything but a job and so we crossed Cook Strait to what, we were told by a man on the ferry, was the 'mainland' — the South Island.

The top of the south was also devoid of opportunities for a middle-aged business man with four dependents, so we headed down the west coast, awed by both the size and quantity of the sandflies that proceeded to devour our fresh northern hemisphere blood with gusto!

Mitch had celebrated his 15th birthday in Rotorua and, learning this was the required age for driving in New Zealand, had pleaded ever since to be allowed behind the wheel. We entered Haast Pass, blithely unaware of what lay ahead, and thought it best to let Mitch drive for the first time on a deserted road. How we ever survived the hairpin turns, twists and sheer drops was a miracle. And, adding to our discomfort, was the fact that we were driving on the opposite side of the road from that to which we were accustomed. It was most definitely a road for the initiated and not one to share with a novice driver.

Recovered from the Haast, we again allowed Mitch to drive as we approached Te Anau. He was feeling more confident now, a view Walt and I did not totally share. Driving on the left-hand side gave me a feeling of displacement and I was forever getting into the driver's side, trying to shift gears with the turn signals and nearly wrenching the gears from their sockets as I tried to indicate a turn. Besides this, I usually wandered to the right of the road staring wide-eyed with fear at the oncoming vehicle and wondering what it was doing on my side of the white line! All in all, I was more of a liability on the road than Mitch who had earned his wings (and at times I thought the whole family's) on the Haast.

Now we were once again in Mitch's hands and nearing Te Anau. Manoeuvring a bend in the road, we came face to face with a mob of bellowing cattle, followed by three men on horseback, hooting, hollering and cracking huge stockwhips. Dogs, with tongues rolling and panting with the chase, snapped and set up a fearful din. Bewildered by what was going on, we stopped and waited to see what would develop. Never had we seen anything like this except in a western film.

One of the cowboys approached us, his spirited horse lathered and rearing, his dogs setting up a continuous chorus. He tipped his hat and, over the din of cattle and dogs, indicated he would clear a space for us to pass through. Whistling and cracking his whip, he did just that, but poor Mitch, a bit unnerved by it all, could only lurch forward and stall, whereupon the cattle quickly filled in the empty spaces, pressing hard against the car.

Still smiling, the cowboy again cleared the cattle away and gave us the go-ahead. A second time we leapt forward and stalled. Unable to hear if the engine was running or not, Mitch fumbled with the keys as the cattle poked their heads in the windows and proceeded to relieve their bowels all over the car.

Patience wearing thin after four abortive attempts, our Roy Rogers made one final attempt to get us out of the way. This time we managed to break clear, followed by several buses, lorries and cars, that roared past us with looks that definitely labelled us as tourists.

In Te Anau we got a motel and tried to explain the condition of the car. 'Could we please have a bucket of soapy water?'

Walt got his first taste of the staying power of cattle and came into the motel with a smell I was soon to become accustomed to. After a shower, we sat down to read the local paper, turning as always to the 'Situations Vacant' column.

'Look!' Walt cried excitedly. 'Shepherd wanted on Government block. Experience preferred but will take someone willing to learn.'

CHAPTER II

Home Is Where The Hearth Is

'Walt, you don't know anything about farming, unless you count washing the cow plops off the car this afternoon,' I chided.

Walt looked at me over his glasses and went to the phone. The next morning we were on our way to meet the manager of the farm and apply for the job.

As the manager strode down the long drive to where we were parked, I noticed something familiar about him. He was none other than the poor cowboy we had so frustrated the day before. I think he recognised our shiny red car about the same time as we recognised him.

'Not a chance of getting this job now,' mumbled Walt under his breath as he got out of the car to take the hand extended to him.

'G'day, I'm the joker in charge here and you're applying for the job, right?'

He was warm, friendly and easy and, in spite of our unorthodox introduction the day before, he hired Walt. The 'Dude' was now a shepherd and we at last had a place to call home after five weeks of wandering around New Zealand.

The next few days were very busy as we raced the 160 kilometres to Invercargill to buy the basic needs for housekeeping. We were absolutely amazed when the kindly manager of the department store suggested we buy second-hand furniture instead of new. The last Americans he had dealt with who had attempted to settle in the shadow of the Takitimus had lasted only three months and they had been forced to sell all their brand-new furniture at a great loss. His thoughtfulness in trying to help us to avoid the same fate was both touching and unnerving. We obviously didn't look like the sort with any 'staying power'. We returned many times after that to report on our progress to this man who took a personal interest in our venture.

Our furniture was delivered in piecemeal fashion. Mary and the boys had beds, but no mattresses, while Walt and I had a lovely double mattress, minus a frame. The kitchen table arrived without chairs and I had an ironing board, but no iron. The fridge was devoid

The ever proud and rebellious Samantha accepts a nuzzle, Samantha along with Jody were my first Arapawa goats and while Jody accepted me totally, Samantha never lost her fierce independence and remained a free spirit.

Philip Leath of Nelson brings a captured doe to safety. Goats were often caught individually when the herd made a break to escape and this one had headed to the sea before she was scooped up and carried back to where the others were waiting.

of shelves and no amount of coaxing would make the vacuum cleaner run.

We finally pulled ourselves and accessories together after a few spirited trips to Invercargill and waited for the first day of work to arrive. Walt left for the job that day all dressed out in jeans, boots and high spirits, only to return at lunchtime looking dejected and forlorn.

'Betty,' he said, 'we've made a terrible mistake.'

I waited, wondering what could possibly have happened in such a short time. 'Don't tell me you got fired already?' I ventured.

He shook his head and, looking grim, burst out: 'No, but I can't understand a word they say! It all sounds the same to me. I listened to them talking for a couple of hours this morning and it might as well have been in Greek!'

After a bite to eat and a wifely pep-talk, he strode off for the afternoon, determined to cope with the 'English accent'.

Meanwhile, I had my own problems. I was amazed from the start at the efficiency of the country housewife and realised that I had a long way to go and many changes to make if I was to measure up.

I soon learned that the 'biscuit tins' were important to the running of the household and played a central part in community life. The tins came in a variety of shapes — round, oblong or square — but they shared the common heritage of being large and always brimming to the top with delicacies of every description. all made by the 'lady of the house'.

Somehow I got the impression that one's achievements were measured by the size of the tin and the diversity of its contents. During the first weeks I met most of the local women and an equal number of biscuit tins, each overflowing with concoctions of chocolate, cream, nuts and pudding mixtures, deliciously blended and looking perfect. On many occasions the visitor would actually leave the full tin as a gesture of welcome, saying she had another at home for her family. This astounded me, for if I had ever managed to create even one of the delights, I would have hidden the tin under the bed and doled out its contents to the family in small quantities over a long period of time.

In addition, the locals' cupboards were bursting with home-made jams and preserves, vying for shelf space with neatly marked jars of preserved fruit and mince. The washing was always blowing on the line hours before I lugged my clothes-basket to the yard. Kitchen floors gleamed as if newly polished no matter what time of day and

I secretly wondered if they mopped after each visitor. I never saw dishes sitting in the sink.

The women were fresh-complexioned, well-groomed and always wore clothes and jerseys they had made themselves. Yet, through it all, they were unpretentious and humble. They totally captivated and amazed me. They found time amidst all this to rear numerous children, help on the farm, tend the chickens, milk the cow and come to make us welcome.

If ever a business wanted to hire an efficiency expert, they could do no better than to employ the rural housewife. I loved them all dearly, but harboured a lasting grudge against the biscuit tins, for they became the mirror that reflected my own inadequacies.

Valiantly I tried to emulate these women but found it impossible. Where dainty, fluffy little pastries sat snuggled in pretty pastel papers in their tins, mine lurched sideways, charred, crumbled and miserable. My chocolate ran and fillings oozed. I had either burnt offerings or underbaked 'soggies' and managed to dirty every dish in the house in the process.

My floor simply would not shine and the bread dough clung to my fingers like wallpaper paste, pulling out into long glutinous strands as I tried to extricate myself. Mountains of farm-stained laundry piled up as I laboured with agitator, wringer, rinsing and hanging. In the States I had put everything in the washer and never looked at it again; the dryer did the rest.

My efforts to conform left me exhausted and frustrated, for I invariably got caught looking frazzled, dishes piled in the sink, footprints everywhere and the washing machine overflowing.

Walt began to comprehend the language somewhat better although he still had to listen carefully. Otherwise he found he had moved the wrong cattle into a neighbour's paddock or that the boss wanted the sheep moved down the road, not across.

On one memorable occasion, Walt got his orders from the manager, leapt into action and sped off in the opposite direction, leaving the manager shaking his head. It was still shaking when Walt returned four hours later with a great mob of unwanted sheep. However, he was improving, although I'm still not sure how the farm fared with all that topsy-turvy moving of stock.

The children had little difficulty in adapting and, although school was not in session when we arrived, they made friends quickly among the young shepherds and neighbours. Roy, the most gregarious, was soon talking about people I hadn't met as old friends, and young

Neville, not much older than Mitch and working on the farm, became a familiar face around the house. So, too, did Tom Brennan, another shepherd. Tom was Maori and his happy-go-lucky ways enchanted and, at times exasperated, us. When Walt and I attended our first function, locally called a 'do', it was Tom who set us at ease in the room full of strangers. The little band was playing but no-one was dancing. The women sat on one side of the room and the men were gathered around a beer keg talking about sheep. I felt keenly aware of every eye as we were the new arrivals and Yanks to boot! Shifting from one foot to the other, I felt a tug on my arm and turning, found Tom who, grinning and already in motion to the beat of the music, said: 'C'mon Betty, let's dance!'

For a split second I hesitated and conflicting thoughts raced through my mind. If I decline, they'll think I'm a racist; if I say 'Yes', I'll be showing off, for the dance floor was still empty.

Throwing my jersey to Walt, I beamed back at Tom and joined him in a wild stomp that made the walls of the woolshed shudder. Before long, everyone was writhing and cavorting. I glanced over at the keg to see Walt in animated conversation and wasn't sure if he was trying to make himself understood by sign language or just being one of the mates, but he was smiling and waving his glass of beer and I assumed all was well. It was a grand evening and gave us the opportunity to meet many of the locals.

We attended several of these get-togethers in various woolsheds and fondly called them 'woolshed-stomps', for many were rowdy and raucous events. The 'stomps' seemed to be the only social life and were held at the drop of a hat and for any reason.

We also had a 'stomp' after shearing. I remember one when it was so warm and sultry that many people had drifted outside to chat. I was talking to a man from Lands and Survey when the doors flew open and out tumbled two men wrestling and jabbing at each other. To my horror, I realised that one of them had a knife. I grabbed Walt's arm and we clung to each other like two monkeys. But those around us never missed a sip of beer or a drag on their cigarettes. In fact, we appeared to be the only ones to notice the life and death struggle going on at our feet.

'Stop them,' I shrieked. 'He's got a knife!'

No one moved or even looked in the direction of the grunting pair.

'Walt, do something,' I begged and he looked at me as if I was crazy.

'Look, lady,' came the voice of a stranger. 'Just relax, it happens all the time. They'll be back drinking together before long.'

I was nearly blubbering with disbelief and still no-one made an effort to intervene, in fact, more people came outside to enjoy the 'entertainment'. Then, as abruptly as it had begun, it stopped and the two men helped each other up and walked arm in arm back into the shed. If this was the local way of solving a disagreement, I wasn't sure I could stand it, but as time went by, we became as blasé about the feuds as the others. It wasn't New York but it was never dull!

Accepting an invitation to one of the more subdued 'dos', we were asked to 'bring a plate'. We interpreted this as meaning that each guest should take his or her own plate, cup, knife, fork, etc., and we proceeded to the hall armed with a fistful of cutlery and dishes. It seemed a reasonable enough request and would mean that no-one would be left with the cleaning-up chores.

Several eyebrows arched and some people lowered their glasses, peering over the tops, when we handed the hostess place settings for two. No-one said anything, but I was aware that all was not quite right.

Walt and I walked uneasily through the twitterings and murmurs, wondering what our latest breach of etiquette had been.

'How quaint,' remarked one well-dressed matron. 'Is that how you do it in America?'

'Do what?' I asked politely. I could tell she wasn't a local — her expensive jersey was not handmade and she didn't bristle her 'r's and swallow her 'a's.

'Do you always carry your dishes and cutlery about with you?' Actually, she said, 'Does one always carry one's cutlery and dishes about with one?'

I was a bit put off by all the 'one's' and was about to tell her it was indeed an old American custom, and that, owing to the dirty water problem, one preferred to wash one's own dishes in one's own water, when the band struck up 'The Gay Gordons' and we were whirled away into a lineup with partners as nimblefooted as elves and we were reduced to a tangle of legs and laughter. I forgot my momentary anger and, while catching my breath, heard a new-found friend's voice whispering in my ear, 'Bring a plate, Betty, means bring something to eat'.

I dutifully brought my 'plate' to the next affair and watched as the cream puffs and mouth-watering pavlovas disappeared around it, leaving my wheatgerm and asparagus loaf a lonely, untouched centrepiece. As the local ladies sat with me over cups of tea, munching politely on one of my latest disasters from the oven, the click, click, click of the knitting needles they took everywhere served to remind me of my own idle hands, by now looking hardened and leathery from encounters with the do-it-yourself life. As I looked at the women who used theirs so productively, my empty hands became an embarrassment. None of them seemed to look at what they were doing, let alone consult the directions.

Undaunted, I purchased a fancy little satchel and filled it with wool, needles and a very basic pattern and embarked on a jersey for Mary. After some late night practice, I felt confident enough to knit two, purl two without concentrating too hard and when the women next gathered in the kitchen, I nonchalantly pulled out my knitting and added my clicking to theirs. No amount of clandestine practice allowed me to drink tea, maintain a conversation and knit at the same time; consequently, I had to undo the wool so many times, it's a wonder the strands held out. When the jersey was finished, the hole for Mary's head was so small she nearly suffocated getting it on and strangled pulling it off. The women assured me they had similar problems, but I knew they could have made the garment in half the time and it would have emerged as a jersey, not a straitjacket!

Shortly after our arrival, the manager suggested to Walt that he muster some rams to eat the grass that was beginning to resemble a jungle in our driveway. The rams were down the road a short way and it should be an easy muster for a beginner.

Walt had acquired two sheepdogs (the previous owner was going to shoot them) and, although he knew nothing about handling dogs and couldn't whistle (an absolute must), we decided to give it a try. It would be a family affair in case Walt needed help.

All five of us, plus the dogs, Mickey and Jack, set off to the paddock, taking the car as a precaution should there be a need for a quick retrieval. Walt opened the gate and tried to imitate the other shepherds he had observed on the block.

'Get away up!' he roared.

Jack and Mickey shot off like rockets while we smiled in appreciation. The smiles turned to shouts of alarm as the dogs ran past the sheep, through the fence and proceeded to disappear from sight. While Walt was busying yelling something that sounded like 'Will he cough' or 'Willie Coe' and which was meant to bring the dogs back, he forgot the gate and the sheep, responding to the shouting and the presence of humans, bolted through and ran like the very devil was after them. Some 50 of them pressed through before we managed to push the gate shut and stem the woolly tide. Leaving the children, we jumped into the car and with some hair-raising driving and fancy footwork, turned them back towards their paddock. The children had the good sense to straddle the road and prevent their escaping in the other direction and they trotted obligingly through the gate.

To get 20 sheep out of 100 and put them where we wanted them to go seemed an impossibility, but this was no time for defeatism.

'Now, we must not be daunted, Walter. Just because the dogs have run off, the sheep are spooked and it's beginning to rain, is no reason to quit. How do the shepherds do it? They send their dogs into the paddock and tell them to bark, right? Well, c'mon kids, we'll be the dogs!'

The children looked at me in astonishment as I dropped on all fours and tried to impersonate a good, keen dog.

'Okay, you guys,' I snarled at the sheep who were ignoring me. 'Woof-woof, Grrrr,' I growled, lunging for added effect.

Oh damn, a car, driving by, slowly. I stood up, brushed off my jeans and smiled thinly at the passers-by. They moved on and I dropped into position again. Mitch joined in the barking and eventually, Mary and Roy came beside me on hands and knees. We lunged and snarled, snapped and barked and eventually the sheep began to take notice and drifted toward the gate.

I looked up to see the same car approaching from the other direction, this time creeping to a halt, its occupants gaping and wide-eyed. Walt stood by the gate, smiling lamely, trying to silence us by flapping his hand wildly behind his back, but we had the sheep on the move now and I wasn't about to stop.

To the complete astonishment of our audience, we barked the sheep through the gate and headed them down the road for the second time. We dashed past the startled onlookers to our car and roared after the galloping mob, overtaking them just in time to guide our grass munchers into the drive. By this time the rain was coming down in buckets and we were soaking wet. The whole exercise had taken four hours and I'm sure sheep have never been mustered in so unconventional a manner. But the means had justified the ends and we had done it ourselves.

While I struggled with my obsession over the biscuit tin, Walt was coping with even more radical changes to his life. His hands grew calloused and the middle-aged paunch began to firm. No longer the well-dressed businessman leaving for work in his big car, he now departed on the back of a truck, surrounded by 20 or so farm dogs, snarling, snapping and cocking their legs in what seemed a deliberate attempt to christen the newcomer.

Occasionally he saddled up Old Mare or Jimmy. Old Mare was devoid of grace and thumped along with stiff and unyielding gait. Jimmy was suffering from a neurosis that would not allow him, under any circumstances, to jump over anything wider than a lunch box. He possessed considerable speed which, combined with his abrupt stops before drainage ditch or culvert, turned Walt into a living catapult. Sailing across the object of Jimmy's phobia, Walt picked himself up, spitting grit and searching for his glasses. Between them, the horses put Walt into Kew Hospital for three weeks as he tried with determination, to learn to ride.

Tony, a fast little pony, became my nemesis when I attempted to join Walt on horseback. This came about when Walt was given the duty of 'lambing' some 2,000 ewes — no small task for one who barely knew one end of a sheep from the other. Most of this work was done on horseback as there were great distances to be covered and any orphans were tucked into the sacks which hung over the horse's rump and brought home for rearing. I was far from comfortable with the prospect of spending a full day in the saddle, but felt Walt might need assistance. So, determined to show the pioneering spirit, I rode off shoulder to shoulder beside my husband in the first glow of dawn.

All went well for the first half of the day and we returned for lunch unscathed. The boys had gone out to play baseball in the paddock while we lingered over coffee discussing the plans for the afternoon. The game was still in progress when we prepared to leave and I was in the process of swinging into the saddle when Mitch hit the ball with a resounding whack and Tony shot off at a run with me dangling from one side, my left foot through the stirrup, and clinging desperately to the saddle. 'Help!' I screamed as we tore across the open spaces and I felt the saddle beginning to slip.

In true rescue fashion, Walt jumped on to Jimmy and came dashing after us. I was absolutely terrified and knew I couldn't hang on much longer, but there seemed no way to stop Tony who by now was in nearly the same state of panic as I was. We were fast approaching a barbed wire fence which could only spell disaster. I could see myself being torn to shreds with my foot caught as it was, and Tony showing no inclination to slow down.

Somehow, I managed to free my foot. At that moment Tony slammed to a halt, reared on his hind legs and, as he touched the earth again, he gave a mighty kick, hurtling me to land on my face, totally unconscious.

The faces of the family swam into focus, all with looks of grave concern. Floating to the surface, I remembered telling the children that if they ever fell from a horse, they should get back on immediately or they might lose their nerve. If I could have moved my mouth, I would gladly have eaten those motherly words of wisdom on the spot. I couldn't tell the kids to do one thing, then change the rules simply because my face resembled that of a boxer who had lost his fight, so, struggling to my feet, I walked stiffly to a quivering Tony and hauled myself aboard.

The remainder of the afternoon was a blur of pain and, far from regaining my nerve, I lost it completely. My neighbour, who had witnessed the accident, rang to see if I was all right. After I assured her that I was only bruised, not broken, she told me she had turned off her television to watch us as it was infinitely better viewing!

Later, I was walking through the paddock barefooted and wearing a sleeveless sundress, when Walt came by on Jimmy. Having recovered some of my nerve, I thought it would be romantic to ride behind him like they do in the movies — hero lifts heroine with one strong arm — and I suggested to Walt we try it. He reached for me with his left arm and I put my unshod foot on the toe of his boot. Jimmy looked back at us and did a quick mental calculation; carrying one dude was bad enough, but he was not going to carry two. With that he began prancing in circles, gaining momentum with each revolution until we were spinning like a giant top. My body was at right angles to Jimmy's when Walt let go and I sailed, arms and legs outstretched, on to the macadam below. As an example of centrifugal force, it was excellent, but I was beginning to feel I should stay earthbound. My neighbour waved to me as I limped past and I wondered what rating she gave the latest performance!

Walt and I had little opportunity to reflect about the newness of our lives but when the chance presented itself, he tried to explain the new terms creeping into his vocabulary such as 'drenching, docking, dagging and dipping', which referred to various techniques in sheep care. If Tarzan and Jane had been 'mates', Walt and I were definitely not — I was the 'old lady' and the only mates Walt had were of the male gender. The local doctor was referred to as 'the Quack' (and was neither incompetent or unqualified!). We no longer sat down to dinner; rather we 'had a feed'. Hogget, thought to be pork, turned out to be year-old sheep meat and colonial goose bore no resemblance to a bird. Food was 'tucker' and the radio was a 'wireless'.

One of the more amusing misunderstandings occurred when we first arrived and the manager asked us if we wanted a house cow or milk in a bottle, and what did we want to do about arrangements for pears? From this we deduced that we had landed in a fruit-growing area and Walt was to be paid partly in pears.

When I asked the manager just what one does with all the pears (having visualised cartons of the things piled in the washhouse awaiting bottling, while the bills went unpaid) he looked at me in amazement.

'What pears are you talking about?' he asked cautiously.

'You know, the ones that come with the house cow or whatever it was.'

'Oh, that. I wasn't talking about pears, I was talking about pear.'

As it turned out, our friend was not talking about fruit at all – he was simply asking us how we wanted to pay our electricity bill. 'Pear' was 'power' and in time we realised when one took a 'shear', one had a 'shower'.

If you asked someone how they felt and they replied, 'A box of birds', it meant all was well; if, on the other hand, they said 'bloody', they were having a bad day. 'Not knowing Arthur from Martha', which sounded like Aatha from Maatha, denoted confusion. When my neighbour's child 'threw a wobbly', she was not aiming a toy at a younger sibling, but having a temper tantrum. An ailing saw was taken to the 'saw doctor' for surgery and a 'panel beater' repaired your car after you 'pranged' it.

On answering the phone, I was invariably asked, 'Are you there?' Obviously I was, or I wouldn't have been on the other end of the line. This normal New Zealand greeting caused me to rupture the caller's ear by shouting, "I'm here, I'm here, can't you hear me?', when all they were saying was our equivalent of 'Hello'.

When invited by some new acquaintances for 'tea' and assuming that to mean cups of tea, cakes and conversation, I said 'Yes' and set the hour for 7.30 p.m. thinking this would allow our hosts plenty of time for their evening meal. We had our own dinner and proceeded to our destination and found ourselves at a table overflowing with 'good kiwi tucker'. We tried gallantly to eat all that was placed before us, giving the children warning kicks under the table and glares that dared them to announce that we had just eaten. The custom, we discovered, was for the hostess to fill each plate and our gracious hostess filled ours to overflowing!

Those years in the rural area were the making and moulding years. Back home, how easy it used to be in time of crisis to call on old friends or relatives; now we called heavily on each other. More importantly, we learned to call on our individual resources. The motto became: 'We can do, we will do, we must do'.

The freezing cold of the house meant the gathering of wood for warmth, quite different from the central heating we had always known. Now we worked to keep warm. After it had been gathered, the wood had to be cut, the fires lit and re-lit. School uniforms had to be sewn (and I barely familiar with needle and thread) and lumps of meat had to be cut into legs, chops and roasts, when all we had ever seen were the neatly wrapped, plastic-sealed packages in the supermarket. It was clear to us that adapting to this new life would not be all sunshine and flowers; we would have to come to grips with many a hard reality. We were fat, happy Americans transplanted to the New Zealand 'wop-wops', hard rough country, full of warm, generous people who accepted life as it came and asked for little.

We were sensitive to those realities of country living and often mistook stoic acceptance for callousness. In some cases, we were right, but most often it was our inexperience that caused a rupture in our otherwise happy existence. Somewhere in those early days, a seed was planted and took root. It grew, slowly, falteringly, surely. It was not the people of the new experiences, both sad and happy, that made the seedling grow. While all of that was enriching, it did not alter our lives as did the feel of the earth between our fingers, the freedom of the open, uncluttered space, the beauty of the mountains and lakes on our doorstep.

We were being drawn towards a deeper appreciation of our surroundings. We were lucky. We had gambled, stepped off into the unknown and been blessed.

Even if it doesn't last, I thought as, for the first time in my 40 years, I watched a little chick hatching, we have gained from it all.

CHAPTER III

In Search Of . . .

Changing countries meant attempting to change habits, attitudes and allegiances. Strangers in Paradise either continually compare the 'homeland' with the 'new land' or strive to conform with a rapidity that makes no allowance for 'old habits to die hard' and can lead to exhaustion, both mental and physical.

This fast-track approach was the one I chose and I launched into community life with the same fervour as I had denounced it in the States. Barely able to balance the family cheque book, I accepted the position of treasurer for the school committee and agreed to assist in the formation of a local theatre group. I immersed myself in bubbling pots of jam and fruit, sewed myself into a pants suit and discussed the virtues of child-rearing with the women in the kitchen, while Walt perused the virtues of sheep-rearing with the men in the lounge. I scrubbed my floors until they gleamed and woke the family by running the 'lux at five in the morning in an effort to prove I wasn't a spoiled American housewife with nothing better to do than watch *'The Young and the Restless'*.

On the social front, I accepted every invitation until my diary read like an appointment book as I flitted from place to place, person to person, running on nervous energy. We questioned nothing, longing to find only good. We had forsaken all; there could be no chink in the armour to let in doubt and hesitation.

Walt took things in his gracious good stride, but for me it had to be right. There was really no need for my frenzy for the kind people of the area accepted us 'warts and all' and many of them became close friends. As a result of their efforts to make us feel at home, we were invited out or had visitors on such a regular basis we had practically no time alone and found ourselves in a whirlwind of activity, almost overwhelmed with kindness.

I remember well the first Easter Sunday. Fearing we would be alone, several families, independent of each other, abandoned their own plans and came to spend the day, resulting in a traffic jam in our driveway and a house bursting with kind intentions!

The distance between the old life and the new broadened as the months rolled by and the ache of homesickness dimmed. We could now hear *White Christmas* and *Chestnuts Roasting by an Open Fire* without getting a catch in our throats and mentally smelling bayberry candles. But letters from the States had assumed a disproportionate importance and I'd rush to meet the mailman each afternoon, praying for a letter. Those were the reassuring echoes of love that kept us in touch with our secure past until we achieved the acceptance of those we had come amongst; a lifeline as we groped to the future.

However, for me, there were some discords in our new life and most of them concerned animals. I soon found that the rural scene was not that pictured in children's farmyard stories and I was not prepared for it. I was not then a vegetarian, but I found the realities of farming on such a large scale made me question my omnivorous heritage.

We had bought a second-hand sauna from a departing American couple and when I saw Walt appear on the horizon with bulging saddlebags, I'd turn it on and have it ready to receive and revive the lambs by the time Walt arrived. After leaving them to 'bake' for ten minutes, we'd try to get them to suckle and the kitchen soon became a foundling home for orphaned lambs with wall to wall boxes of bleating babies. Many hours were spent preparing formulas, feeding, cleaning and burying those that didn't respond. We couldn't pass any lamb that looked even vaguely distressed and brought home many it would have been kinder to have killed on the spot.

I wept when these little creatures were taken away and loaded on to a truck headed for the abattoir and was never able to harden myself to their intended fate. I found myself rejoicing when they died rather than when they recovered.

On one occasion, as I was driving down the road, I saw a lamb in the throes of death and pleaded with my companion, a farmer, to alleviate its suffering. He stepped over the fence, picked up the lamb by its back legs and before my eyes proceeded to bash its brains out against a post! That wasn't quite what I had in mind, but it was, it seemed, the way of the land.

Other things contributed to a growing restlessness; one being the impermanence of living in a Lands and Survey home that was soon to be balloted off, along with the land, to some aspiring young farmer. That meant we couldn't really establish ourselves and begin the lifestyle we sought.

Another problem was the apparent lack of opportunity for the children once they left school. They had settled into the little school in Hydro Village, a temporary settlement for those engaged on the Manapouri power project. The mixture of students was cosmopolitan, although they looked strangely alike in the gray and blue uniforms.

Mitch rebelled at wearing shorts, the standard apparel for all seasons, and covered his gangling adolescent legs with longs.

Having determined I would make Mary her school dress, I sought a pattern at the shop only to be informed there were none.

'Oh,' I tried to sound casual, 'then how do you go about making the uniforms?'

'We just cut the pattern from an old one.' And I knew the gauntlet had been flung.

'That sounds easy enough,' I lied.

Had I swallowed my pride and paid someone to make it, Mary might not have had to be literally sewn into her dress the day school began but as it was, she stood with arms raised as I sewed a spare piece under each arm so that the dress would encircle her completely. I advised her not to make any unnecessary movements or breathe too deeply, lest she find herself devoid of covering.

The children returned from that first day with many tales to tell. Mitch's class began with the headmaster entering the room, whereupon the students leapt to their feet, leaving Mitch seated and bewildered. This homage to superiors was unknown in the schools he had attended in America, but once the custom was explained, he genuflected on cue with the rest. Mary had remained as immobile as circumstances allowed and had not begun to fray until mid-afternoon. The kids in the class had been friendly and curious.

Invited on to the field, the boys joined in a game of rugby which they could only describe as an Indian massacre and a decidedly unhealthy way to stay healthy.

They studied Mother England and New Zealand's allegiance to her, as well as the sovereign independence from her, and parliamentary democracy as Keith Holyoake won his fourth victory. They relearned the alphabet from A to 'Zed' and Rs were dropped altogether. Car sounded like Caa and card was cad. Any word that ended with an 'a' assumed an invisible 'r'; Cuba became Cuber, Canada, Canader, and Australia, Australier. In reverse our pronounciation of farm sounded to the New Zealanders like forum and a dog was a dawg. However, the kids soon worked it out and cut the communication gap far faster than Walt who was still mustering the neighbour's sheep.

In spite of a daily schedule that left little time for reflection, I felt in limbo, much as I had before we came to New Zealand. Walt was annoyed; was I never to be satisfied, always chasing rainbows and tilting at windmills? He had worked hard to settle us in and now I was insisting we move on. He refused to discuss any change unless there was a job and home to go to, for his was the responsibility of providing and the children had had enough insecurity. He thought that would be the end of the matter as obtaining a second job would be impossible after his difficulties with the present one.

However, deep inside, I knew Southland was the prelude to an unwritten song. Whether it would be joyful or melancholy I didn't know, but I did know it was time for the first chord. We would bide a while longer, but we would not stay.

Walt had not had a holiday, unless we counted the time spent in traction in Kew Hospital when Old Mare and Jimmy combined their talents and left him with weights dangling from each foot. It was a very painful experience for him and exhausting for the family as we made the 300-kilometre round trip to Invercargill to visit him.

It was on one of these trips that our cat, Malama, made her incredible journey. I had made the trip alone that day, staying as long as possible with Walt to help him wile away the hours in his immovable position, then stopped in town for some shopping before starting home in the pouring rain. As I drove into the garage where the boys were working, Roy raised his hands in alarm, yelling: 'The cat!' Oh no, I've run over her, I thought and buried my face in my hands, lowering them as I heard the plaintive meow of a very much alive cat. All I could see was the bonnet of the car the boys had lifted open. I jumped out in time to see Roy lifting Malama (covered in oil and mud) from under the right front fender. She had been in the habit of crawling in to curl up next to the warm motor and must have been asleep when I started the car in the morning. From her condition, and the fact that none of the children had seen her all day, there was no doubt she had been under the fender for the entire day, perhaps too frightened to jump clear. Just why she chose not to abandon ship when the car was parked at the hospital and in town, we had no way of knowing. Perhaps she knew she would be lost forever and, with an intelligence unknown to us, had understood she must stay where she was. There was great jubilation as we cleaned and brushed her matted hair to its silver perfection and prepared a meal fit for such a bold and fearless feline.

Walt was finally discharged and graduated to a back brace. Despite obvious pain, he gamely saddled up again, his girdle holding his vertebrae firmly in place. It was decided we both needed a change after the fairly intensive programme of integration in our adopted country and a rest would assist in Walt's recovery. It would give us the opportunity to combine business with pleasure and I suggested we head for the north of the South Island and, while there, look for employment. I set about making arrangements for the children and animals during our absence while Walt put in extra hours in order not to inconvenience the other shepherds while we were away.

Walt was sitting astride Jimmy, waiting for Tom to clear the paddock of sheep before admitting the cows and calves. The animals milled about, the dogs keeping them from straying, and it was this colourful scene of rural activity that attracted a passing tour bus from which clambered 40 or so excited American tourists with cameras at the ready.

Walt was done up in jeans, boots and an Australian cowboy hat sent by a friend, and he presented quite a picture. He sat proud in the saddle, simply because his girdle was killing him, the unyielding bones in the thing causing him to sit straight and tall! The picture was completed with a prancing horse, obedient dogs, milling cattle and the snow-capped Takitimus in the background.

'Let's get a picture of a gen-u-ine Noo Zealand cowboy,' trilled a plump little woman in tight pink slacks. She started photographing Walt from various angles and he complied by smiling and pushing his hat into a jaunty position, like the Marlboro Man.

It all went well until they began seeking conversation. Not wishing to disappoint them with his Yankee twang, Walt answered in clipped monosyllables: 'Yep!' 'Nope!' and the occasional 'I reckon', gave a reasonable impression of the strong, silent type.

Getting a bit carried away, he relaxed his hold on the reins to doff his hat, leaning on the pommel of the saddle for added effect as the satisfied tourists prepared to leave. Sensing Walt's momentary distraction, Jimmy, not about to be upstaged, started a performance of his own and it was with great difficulty that Walt reined him in.

This lively finale brought squeals of admiration from the women as Walt demonstrated his prowess on horseback. He got away with the charade and no doubt Walt and Jimmy adorn many a photograph album under the caption 'Cowboy of New Zealand'.

A friend offered to stay with the children so, equipping the American Buick we had brought with us to tow the rented caravan, Walt, our three terriers and I headed north.

Walt was now better prepared for job interviews. He had almost conquered the language barrier, had some skills in shepherding and looked the part with his lean and weathered countenance. However, after two weeks of leisurely camping and intensive job searching, we had nothing better to show for our efforts than the offer of a position on a tobacco farm in Nelson. The prospects for change were not looking good, and to round out the holiday, the car broke down.

Finding the necessary parts for an American car proved impossible so an urgent cable was sent to my brother in the States requesting bits and pieces to get the Buick moving again. We were told that we could expect no reply for at least three days, so we parked the caravan and rented a van advertised as a 'Home Away From Home'. It sounded cosy but it refused to accommodate Walt's 1.8 metres and he was reduced to sliding around the interior on his bottom. The sink was the size of a saucepan and the water pump didn't work. The two side benches folded out to make a bed and required an agility neither of us seemed to possess, for our efforts to make the bed in such confined quarters (with the three terriers) reduced us to gales of laughter as we sat in a jumble of sheets, blankets, pillows and yapping terriers who thought the whole exercise was for their entertainment.

Apart from all that, the van shook violently, leaving us in worse condition than after a session on Old Mare and did nothing to assist in Walt's recovery. It was, however, all that was available so we shuddered off in the direction of Golden Bay. The beauty of the area had been described to us and it seemed an ideal time to go as we waited for the reply from the States. The drive provided a panorama of loveliness with breathtaking views. However, also in sight was a large sign that warned 'No dogs allowed unless dosed for hydatids in the last 28 days'. Alas, our three wee terriers did not meet the criteria and, disappointed, we turned around and rattled back to Blenheim.

Our little Chitty Chitty Bang Bang was bid a welcome farewell after three days' forced confinement and we headed for the garage only to be told that the parts for the Buick would not arrive in New Zealand for at least three months.

The entire South Island separated us from home and the rented caravan had to be in Te Anau in two days as the owner had it booked and we had given a firm assurance on the matter. Looking at our bank balance after the purchase of a second-hand car with tow-bar made us a bit uneasy, but we had no choice. The Buick would have to stay as we had a deadline to meet.

Having sorted out that problem, we strolled the streets of Blenheim late in the afternoon.

Mike Willis of Willowbank Wildlife Reserve of Christchurch, the man responsible for organizing the first three musters to save the goats gently lowers a goat into the dinghy to be ferried out to the Moonraker.

Each goat was carefully handled aboard admist a throbbing sea that demanded a delicate balancing act. Outstretched arms brought the goats to the decks of the Moonraker.

Greg Crisp trying to outwit and outrun a young buck bent on swimming back to England rather than be captured. The outcome was predictably wet, but safe for man and goat.

Malama . . . our first animal friend in New Zealand. It was this persistent puss who thrice brought the beleagured pigeon to our doorstep and Leroy's lap as he teetered upon the bucket.

'Walt,' I said suddenly. 'Let's go to the land agent.'

'Whatever for?'

'To see if there are any farms for sale.'

Stopping short and raising his hands in an expression of defence, Walt gave an emphatic 'No' and launched into all the reasons he was not prepared to follow up this preposterous suggestion. While he listed his lack of experience, expertise and finance as three excellent excuses for not taking the matter any further, I was leading him towards Dalgetys.

Walt can be as sweet as an Irish song, but he can also be as stubborn as any mule and getting him up the steps, through the door and into the agent's office took a lot of sweet talking and cajoling while physically pulling him by the arm, which he didn't resist for fear of creating a scene.

He sat with a look of total disdain as the agent showed us a number of properties in Marlborough and a few in the Sounds, all well and truly out of our price range. There would be no mortgage *if* we ever decided to buy a place. Walt felt he was beyond assuming a mortgage at his age and it would be cash or nothing.

The 'I told you so' expression changed when the agent mentioned a property in East Bay, Queen Charlotte Sound, and pointed to a tiny dot on the map. It was small, the house needed repairs, fences — not too bad, right on the water and, oh yes, there had been a small slip at the rear of the house. Best of all, the price was right.

I fairly danced out the door already picturing us living like Crusoe and Friday. Walt remained, as ever, with his feet on the ground, while I, head in the clouds, twittered in ecstacy. He reminded me that we hadn't even seen the place nor were we likely to. We had to leave for Te Anau the next morning. I speculated on the chances of persuading Walt to delay our departure in favour of the trip to East Bay, but decided that might stretch my luck and Walt's temper a bit thin and had to be satisfied with the agent's promise to ring us if he heard of any jobs or if the property was sold.

Back in Te Anau we resumed life at the same frantic tempo with Walt chasing sheep and me chasing a basketball. A little woman from Scotland, whose husband was with the Manapouri project, and I were asked to join the women's basketball team. Neither of us had ever played, nor had an interest in the game. We warned the matrons on the team that we'd be no asset, but it seemed some championship game was pending and our local team was short of two players. Without Marny and me they couldn't qualify and they pleaded their case so vigorously, we finally relented. It just might be fun!

It turned out the 'big game' was to take place in exactly three days and I wondered at our chances of becoming Harlem Globetrotters at such short notice. Marny and I were put through a two-day crash course, the women taking turns at teaching us the finer points of their sport. At the end of the second day I was so exhausted, I could barely lift the ball, let alone run around the court with it and still had only the vaguest idea what the game was about. If the game's outcome rested with Marny and me, the team might as well concede defeat and forget the whole thing.

Plump and skinny posteriors encased in blue gym-slips; blue-veined legs and housemaids' knees radiant above socks and sneakers, we paraded on to the floor to meet the foe. Some of the women bounced the ball menacingly as we eyed up our opposition. There was a lot of knee-bending, flexing, stretching and 'Go-get-'ems' with everyone in a state of high tension. It really didn't look as if we were shaping up for a game of fun.

I've never experienced such stage fright as I did on the evening of my sporting debut for I knew I'd be watched to see if I barked or dribbled as the story of our good keen dog escapade had made its way around town. Aside from the slight chance I'd be in the right place once we started running around the court, my heart sank to see the number of people that had turned out for the event; the hall was packed, locals on one side, visitors on the other.

Someone gave me an unladylike shove and we ran, middle-aged and grim, on to the court. I remember very little of the first round, except that Marny and I seemed to end up at one end of the room, with everyone else at the other. The referee, who nearly blew his brains out, whistled at our mistakes. At half-time no one spoke to us except our husbands who delivered pep talks like trainers to prizefighters.

Back we went, dodging, diving and grabbing. Suddenly, to my complete astonishment, the ball hit me in the stomach and came to rest in my outstretched arms. It might well have been a red-hot brick. Remembering something about not holding the ball and bouncing it when you ran, I hopped, skipped and tippy-toed down the hall in a dazzling display of footwork, endeavouring to rid myself of the object that unfortunately followed obediently along beside me. There didn't seem to be anyone near, friend or foe, to throw the damned thing to, so I kept hopping and bouncing. I must have dazzled the opposition and team-mates alike into a momentary state of paralysis for all action on the court seemed to have stopped except my cat-on-a-hot-tin-roof performance. Then, like a herd of stampeding cattle, both teams bore down on me and I recalled Mitch's Indian massacre.

One well-developed woman, the unchallenged champion of the opposition, puffed up to me and snarled: 'So you want to play dirty, do you?'

No, I didn't want to play dirty, in fact I didn't want to play at all and I hadn't the foggiest notion what I was doing.

She lunged for the ball while in desperation I spun on one foot deflecting the snatch. It was a sheer fluke, but now the battle lines were drawn and I began receiving discreet but numerous scratches, pinches and body blows as we wove in and out around the floor.

It seemed to go on and on and I had no idea what the score was. As the game reached fever pitch, I again got in the path of the ball. This time I spotted Marny standing alone and quickly threw it to her. Her first reaction was that of a startled doe. Then her competitive instincts took over and, seeing one end of the court clear, she hugged the ball to her bosom, running like something possessed and with a triumphant howl, proceeded to bag a hole-in-one — in the opposition's basket!

With this, the game was declared well and truly over with the opposition, locals and referees alike muttering to themselves and shaking their heads at the Scottish-American alliance that rewrote Manapouri basketball.

Fortunately, the game was not held against me and I soon regained the good graces of the sporting matrons. Marny and I teamed up on another occasion when she asked me to teach her to drive. We proved almost as dangerous on the highway as we did on the basketball court and Marny's husband called a halt to the lessons when Marny drove through the garage door with her instructor by her side.

Since returning from our holiday, I had been more restless than before despite all the distractions of daily life. I dreamed of a Shangri-la I hadn't seen and nagged Walt constantly about moving. He was immovable. The five weeks we had spent living like gypsies when we first arrived remained firmly in his mind.

Some months went by, then came a call from the agent in Blenheim. True to his word, he had news of a position available in Pelorus Sound and yes, the property was still on the market. Since Walt was unable to take any more time off, it was decided that I would make the journey instead. The family dropped me at Gore station where I took the night train to Christchurch and from there a bus to Blenheim.

Arriving totally exhausted, I booked a room at Barry's Hotel and went straight to bed.

I found my transportation to Pelorus would be by the mail launch that delivers mail and supplies twice a week to the remote sound. The boat left about 8 o'clock and by 1.30 p.m. I had reached my destination and was greeted on the wharf by the family I hoped would soon be our employers.

I answered all their questions about Walt's abilities with assurance — he could 'do anything' — praying he wouldn't be called upon for a task he wasn't prepared for should they hire us. It must have seemed strange to them — an American woman arriving out of the blue, promising her husband could make cheese of the moon and negotiating for a job, while he was at home baby-sitting! Nevertheless, we were offered the position which I accepted on the spot.

'Start packing!' I directed over the phone when I rang Walt to tell him he now had a six-month contract to be carpenter extraordinaire among other things. 'It's all systems go.'

The next morning the agent, the owner of the property and his little daughter, picked me up at the hotel and we drove through to Picton from where we set off in the direction of East Bay and Aotea. I was about to see if dreams really do come true.

The day was one of exquisite beauty. A sky of vivid blue, cotton-candy clouds drifting over the hilltops, the water serenely green and gulls making lazy circles in the sky above us. As far as the eye could see were the interwoven hills and bays of the sound, dotted here and there with cottages, boats bobbing on the moorings.

Sitting quietly at the back of the boat, I pictured Aotea for the hundredth time. Such was my preoccupation, I didn't notice one of the passengers had joined me and I was woken from my reverie by loud slurping noises. Looking up, I saw my companion was the owner's daughter who was lustily devouring mussels raw from their shells. She smiled when she felt my eyes on her and offered me some of the delicacy, which I declined. Watching as she relished her gourmet delight from the sea, her golden curls kissed by the sun, I shuddered despite the warmth of the day.

'What's the matter?' asked the child.

'Nothing, darling,' I reassured here. It's just that it's all so beautiful that I hope it never changes.'

How could I say to this child of the sun that we must cherish and hold dear the wonders of the natural world, that she was such a lucky little girl to grow up amidst such beauty and it would be for her and those of her generation to guard and protect it from the mistakes and folly of my generation. That she must learn to walk gently on the earth and leave no scar.

We had seen beautiful lakes turned to sewers and wild places laid waste. We had witnessed the ravages of pollution and over-population but when we spoke to New Zealanders about them, they would casually reply that it couldn't happen here. But the day was too glorious and the child too innocent to dwell on such dark thoughts. We chatted away and she solemnly instructed me in the art of removing the hairy bits from the mussels and why they shouldn't be eaten. Then she fell contentedly asleep in the sun.

My excitement increased as we neared East Bay and I was almost brimming over when we finally pulled into the rather spindly jetty, which led to a woolshed, its boards flapping a plaintive welcome in the breeze. My first impression of Aotea was that everything seemed to be falling down or at best leaning at a precarious angle and the little house looked grey and unloved as it struggled for sunlight amidst the tangle of supplejack and honeysuckle that surrounded it. The hills were covered with scrub and the refuse-choked stream running beside the house could hardly be called a burbling brook. Inside, the ceiling hung from the rafters and the wallboard from the frame. Hardened candlewax adorned windowsills and benchtops alike and the interior was musty and cold despite the warm sunshine outside. And a ton of earth had parted company with the hillside and slammed into the back of the house leaving a mountain as high as the roof.

I felt an overwhelming sense of disappointment, for it was nothing like I had pictured it in my fanciful dreams. I opened the door, hoping the shaft of sunlight would brighten both the kitchen and my mood. Stepping on to the concrete landing and surveying the ailing sheds and fences, I failed at first to notice the little bird hopping about my feet. His persistent antics quickly turned my frown upside down and I felt he was beckoning me to follow. As I stepped into the sun, through the sheepyards and out along the track, the true beauty of Aotea unfolded before me.

The green hills stood in sharp contrast with the blue of the sky and I filled my nostrils with sweet, clean air. Below, the sea lapped a gentle lullaby against the rocks and gulls scolded at my intrusion, A soft wind played timidly with the collar of my jacket, its fingers warm and caressing.

Looking back towards the house as we prepared to leave, I blew a kiss to the little bird and whispered 'Thank you'. The tiny creature spread its tail like an exquisite oriental fan and danced up and down the branches of the tree and I knew I hadn't dreamed in vain. A troupe of performing dolphins escorted us to Picton, frolicking and cavorting, their fixed smiles in place, as the child and I laughed and clapped with delight. They brought more magic to an already enchanted day.

Walt gave the required two weeks' notice and once more the boxes and suitcases were packed and the round of goodbyes began. Our friends gave us a farewell party that touched us deeply. The farewells were not as traumatic as when we left the States, but they were sad. These lovely people had befriended us during those first fragile months and helped us on our way. Now it was time to go.

We drove slowly past the homes of polished floors, bulging cupboards and generous hearts, pausing at the paddocks where we had laboured to save ewes and lambs on freezing southern nights. Velvety noses nudged and nuzzled when we stroked the horses for the last time, all offences on both sides forgiven. Laughter finally overcame sadness when we passed the paddock of the 'good, keen dogs'.

The snow-capped Takitimus thrust upwards into the blue void above and in their serene permanence looked down upon the restless mortals, winding their way through the foothills in search of other mountains and other places and watched with benign indifference until we were out of sight.

Mitch, Walt and I had been sharing the driving and my turn came up when we reached Balclutha. As we started the ascent leading from the town several hundred sheep appeared on the horizon, barrelling down the road and heading straight for us. I stopped halfway up the hill to allow them to pass.

'Okay, let's go,' instructed Walt as the last of the woollies trouped by.

'I don't think I can do it with all the weight on behind,' I said, referring to the trailer loaded with dogs and assorted cartons and viewing the long line of traffic behind us. All thoughts of coordination left me and I knew I'd never make the brakes, gears, clutch and accelerator function at the same time. 'Walt, I know I can't do it.'

I was quite willing at that moment to succumb to the 'men-are-superior' adage and play the helpless female but Walt refused to be gallant and launched into detailed instructions as to what I should do and how I should do it.

'Okay,' I snapped, 'don't say I didn't warn you!' And, with a mighty roar, hands and feet fairly flapping, we lurched . . . backwards. The only sound was the tinkle, tinkle of what had been the left headlight of the car behind.

With a sigh and the look of a long-suffering spouse, Walt walked to the agitated couple in the Mini and proceeded to apologise for his wife's ineptitude, promising to do better and to pay for any damage I had caused.

He returned to the driver's seat where I sat gripping the wheel and staring straight ahead. 'Move over.' And he sidled into the spot I had happily vacated.

We were now ready for take-off and, indicating that I should watch how it ought to be done, a look of male supremacy on his face, he hit the accelerator.

Tinkle, tinkle, tinkle . . . the car behind was now minus two headlights! The children sat like 'hear no evil — see no evil — speak no evil', aware that any comment at this particular time would not be in their best interests. I had to fight hard to suppress my profound pleasure at the justice that had been done. The couple in the Mini were understandably annoyed and although we gave them our address, they never contacted us, presumably only too glad to be rid of us once and for all.

It was raining heavily when we reached Kaikoura and, pulling up fourth in a line of cars halted by a huge landslip, we awaited the arrival of the Ministry of Works. Many more cars piled up behind us as we waited seven hours in the cold and damp for a track to be cleared. Besides ourselves, we had the three terriers and Fred, the cat, and they all had to be taken out to relieve themselves at intervals. We backed the car under an overhang to give the dogs in the trailer some protection. The seven hours seemed an eternity, the cold penetrating to the bone. However, as with all things, it came to an end, and we moved on through a river of mud, each car in the line spraying the one behind with waves of brown water left in its wake.

It was 3.30 in the afternoon when we rang our new employer from Blenheim to say we were on our way. There was hesitation on the other end, then: 'Do you think you can make it!'

With only 100 kilometres to go and several hours of daylight left, of course we could make it and we rang off with a cheery 'See you soon'.

Our optimism faded quickly when we were reduced to travelling 40 kilometres an hour over Queen Charlotte Drive, a road that snakes its way through Kenepuru Sound and which six hours later led us to the turn-off for Pelorus Sound. Darkness had overtaken us and so had the rain, cascading in sheets, blown by a howling wind. A light from a distant farmhouse was all that could be seen in the otherwise ebony night. The turn-off road was the width of one car and we climbed slowly up the steep incline, which had now become slippery and dangerous. The car laboured through ruts and mud and slid ominously from side to side, the trailer adding to our instability.

A wall of earth loomed up in the beam of the headlights and Walt slammed on the brakes, slithering to a stop centimetres from the slip that blocked the entire road. We had been on the road for some 30 hours and were bone weary, with our stamina at low ebb, and it took several minutes to come to grips with this latest obstacle and get the adrenalin flowing. The first thing we had to attend to was the trailer, its weight threatening to pull us from our muddy perch. I sat pressing my foot hard on the brake and gripping the handbrake, while in the darkness the family searched for rocks to place behind the rear wheels. They unhitched the trailer and guided it into the side of the hill, consoling the dogs who, by now, were drenched and miserable. Mary, Fred and I huddled together for warmth as Walt and the boys groped towards the farmhouse we had passed.

Knocking on the door, Walt wondered if he'd be met by the barrel of a shotgun, for it seemed a very desolate and deserted spot and the occupants wouldn't be expecting visitors on such a night. Instead, he was met by a shovel and the understatement of the year: 'Having a bit of bother out there?'

Mary and I must have dozed off for we were woken by grating sounds as the men tried to dig through the wall of earth. Using any tool to hand, we all dug and clawed at the slip but our small displacements of earth were barely visible.

Although the situation was far from funny, I got the giggles.

'Maybe you'd better go back to the car,' said Walt, thinking the strain had been too much.

'No, I'm all right, really. It's just that I can't believe this is happening. It's unreal. No-one will ever believe we're doing what we are doing.'

Laughter can be infectious even in totally impossible circumstances and before long we were all singing.

'All I want is a room somewhere, Far away from the cold night air,' bawled Roy.

'Oh, the weather outside is frightful, but the fire is so delightful, and since we've no place to go, let it rain, let it rain, let it rain!' Our friends in the farmhouse must have thought 'spirits' were abroad in the night as they heard the strains of *'Singing in the Rain'* floating from the mountain road. We broke through the slip just as we were toting the barge and lifting the bale of *'Old Man River'* and having determined beforehand to leave the trailer since we could never start with the added weight, we jumped into the car and, with spinning wheels, lurched ahead. The dogs howled in protest at this desertion, but desperate situations demand desperate action.

We slid to a halt next to a man holding a torch and leaning against a Landrover. The son of our new employer kindly offered to rescue our dogs, whereupon he and Walt jumped into the Landrover and headed back to the trailer. You could almost hear the canine sigh of relief when the vehicle's lights came around the bend. However, our journey was not yet over for, from the main house, we had to battle a further kilometre through a quagmire to our cottage. We mumbled something incoherent to our new employers about a rough trip, dried and fed the dogs and literally stumbled into unmade beds, clothes and all.

A bright and clear dawn greeted us and, despite the fatigue of three days' difficult travel, we were up early to inspect our new surroundings and found them beautiful. Crail Bay seemed very isolated to us at the time but was to serve as a training ground for the future.

It was a very different life indeed from that in Te Anau and a world away from that in the States. Mr and Mrs Menzies were charming. Walt did his best to meet their requirements, which involved very little stock work and a great deal of carpentry. The children now took on a new challenge, that of Correspondence School work. All their lessons were mailed to them and then returned for marking and suggestions by a teacher they never saw. This unique learning process taught them discipline and self-reliance and left them with time to absorb other things of interest not always found in textbooks.

We explored the shore and surrounding hills, watched the dolphins play on our doorstep and chuckled at the cheeky wekas trying to steal the cat's dinner on the front porch. Walt hammered away for the Menzies and the boys painted a nearly cottage. Mary, Fred and I took walks, following the tracks into the hills or along the shore. Fred roamed the beaches with me, chasing the teasing gulls, while I let the little waves try to outwit my toes as they chased my footprints in the sand.

Evenings were spent by the fire, planning and dreaming, talking and reading the books that lined the walls of the cottage. It was a time to reflect and come to terms with isolation. I wondered if we were enough for each other. Without the diversions of television, social life and people to fill the void, could we sustain one another? What would our chances be if Aotea became a reality instead of a dream?

During one of my walkabouts with the three terriers, Tiki, Piko and Mike, I chanced upon a cow giving birth. She had chosen, as her place of delivery, a very steep incline that fell into a deep stream. We sat on a distant knoll watching the miracle unfold until the mother's vigorous lickings sent the tottering newborn tumbling into the stream below. The calf struggled to its feet in the icy water, but was unable to climb out. I clambered to the side of the stream and bent to lift the infant, already the size of a dog, on to the dry land. The next instant I was hit by a ton of fury, bent on my destruction. The irate mother ran over me from the left, then turned to have another go.

I was in no position to argue and, without a moment's hesitation, I rolled myself into the stream beside the calf to avoid the next onslaught. I pleaded, cajoled and threatened to have her made into instant hamburger, but she refused to allow me to venture near her calf. So I waded downstream far enough to come ashore safely and set off for the homestead and help. The cow, knowing and trusting the Menzies family, allowed the calf to be lifted from the stream and he ducked dripping and hungry under Mum for a well-deserved drink. I waited around long enough to see the pair reunited, then hobbled home to nurse my bruises, which were considerable. I was very thankful Mama didn't have horns or I may not have survived my mission of mercy.

Three months passed before we could arrange a trip to see Aotea and when the day finally arrived, it was cold and grey and we were escorted not by dolphins, but by a stiff southerly wind that made two of the children seasick. I watched for the family's response, which was unanimous — no-one was impressed and sideways glances between them told me they were thinking I'd done it again with tales of magic birds and enchanted dolphins. Walt remained ominously silent, always a bad sign, especially when he produced a groan on walking to the back of the house and seeing the landslide.

Things weren't going too well and I looked about in vain for that jolly fantail and made chirruping sounds to call him. That made the family view me with renewed alarm. Indecision etched Walt's face and I knew what his thoughts must be. We weren't pioneers, nor even slightly experienced in self-sufficiency. We would be miles from everywhere and everyone with nothing to guide us but our city-bred instincts and a copy of the *'Mother Earth Almanac'*. It wasn't much on which to base our future.

As if on cue, the clouds parted above the hills and unveiled to the family the Aotea I had seen, this time crowned with a glorious rainbow. The sun glistened on the wet grass and the trees gave off shimmering little diamonds of light, quickly dispelling any lingering shadows.

We walked along the track where the bird had led me and beauty cast her spell. When Walt stopped, surveyed the hillside, then said: 'We'll have to put a fence here', I knew he had made his decision.

CHAPTER IV

Life at Aotea

Aotea . . . a homestead on an island, a long way from everything, secluded, wildly beautiful. Yes, I laid it on heavily when I wrote to the family in the States about it. Condescendingly, I reminded them that we had done what so many say they want to do — we had got away from it all. We had even managed to find our Shangri-la on an island, free from noise, congestion and pollution. No more the 9-5 rat race. We'd wash our clothes in the stream, drink goats' milk and grow rosy and heathly on organically-grown vegetables. The men would hunt for meat in the wilds of the island's mountain tops. We were, I wrote smugly, about to take up the castaway existence so many disenchanted Americans talk and dream about, but seldom manage to achieve.

It all sounded terribly romantic and courageous, full of bravado. Perhaps now that the eleventh hour was approaching, I was trying to convince the family that, like Joseph Smith and his band, we had found the promised land.

Pride goeth before a fall, so they say, and the romance was soon replaced with the reality and the bravado with humble acceptance of our shortcomings and lack of knowledge. It had all looked so delightful in the movie *Swiss Family Robinson*, but this was no movie set and Aotea was to become the edge that sharpened our nebulous and idealistic attitudes towards the do-it-yourself life. We fulfilled the six-month contract with the Menzies, the time dragging as we inched our way to the day we set sail for Aotea. With the exception of an axe, shovel and blankets, and a meagre amount of food, everything else was loaded aboard a punt to be brought to the island the following day. Dogs, cats, children and two starry-eyed adults boarded our newly-purchased boat, *Sirius*, and pushed off in the direction of Arapawa Island.

We must have presented quite a sight; the little boat laden down with its curious cargo of Americans in search of Paradise. Fred sat confidently at the ship's wheel while the other two cats cried plaintively in their boxes. The dogs, unused to sea travel, fought to gain their footing on the rolling decks. We nosed into the jetty as the sun was dipping behind the hill across the bay. The animals were released amidst a flurry of yelps, barks and hisses; the cats happy to be free of their confinement raced to the nearest tree and remained there, while the dogs ran about investigating and christening their new surroundings.

Hurriedly we unloaded the few things we had brought and made our way to the house. Walt quickly built a fire, while the rest of us searched for candles. We topped off a meal of bread, fruit and cheese with a toast of wine brought for the occasion, clinking glasses and looking for suitable words to mark our arrival. It all seemed slightly bizarre, sitting in the semi-darkness, falsely animated, lamely making efforts at conversation with a cheerfulness we did not feel, the light from the candles casting strange shadows on the dilapidated walls and dangling cobwebs. The atmosphere was unfriendly and unwelcoming. We spoke awkwardly, trying not to show the doubts we were experiencing, until, mercifully, the candles burned low, allowing us the privacy of pretended sleep.

To add to the general atmosphere of gloom, the darkness closed in around us as the fire died out. The branches scratched across the windows like fingernails on a chalkboard. No bird of paradise sang for us that night, only the morepork with its eerie, rhythmic hoot. The clouds vaulted the sky, covering and uncovering the moon, briefly illuminating the room, then plunging us once more into darkness. The house seemed full of things that go bump in the night. Floorboards creaked and groaned under some invisible weight and the sighs from the little house brought to mind stories of the Maori spirits that restlessly roam the island.

Daybreak brought relief from the mosaic of sound and imagination and we rose to the first day at Aotea. A cup of tea was definitely the first priority, much needed to shake off the fatigue of a sleepless night and with this in mind, we approached the little wood stove sitting disconsolately beneath several layers of grease and grime. This creature of a bygone era might as well have been a modern-day computer. It looked terribly complicated to work with all the doors and things one opened to regulate the heat. Locating the firebox, we set the fire, lit a match and immediately discovered what our first job would be, for great billowing clouds of eye-stinging smoke rolled into the kitchen, sending us diving for the door, eyes streaming.

By taking turns with 'Little Bertha', as we christened her, we finally produced a cup of tea which we drank on the front step to escape her rude belches of smoke. Obviously Bertha had had a lifetime of smoky digressions and since she was to be our source of heat, hot water and cooking, something had to be done to tame her. Mary and I coaxed Bertha into heating a few buckets of water and set to cleaning her grubby exterior. Several hours later, hands and face smudged with black, we sat back to appreciate the results of our efforts. Bertha's tan exterior shone and she looked quite a respectable relic.

There were enough beds in the house to open a hotel and these were carried to the woolshed. Old wallpaper and linings were torn away and a wall demolished to enlarge the room we had decided would be the lounge. Mary and I followed the demolition crew armed with buckets and scrubbing brushes and scrubbed everything in sight. So intent were we on making the house ready for the arrival of the furniture, we had not noticed the change in the weather. Only when we sat down amidst the chaos for a bite to eat did we realise the sea had become a carousel of white caps and the sky a dark canopy. We had no telephone and had simply to hope that the punt would arrive as expected. However, the wind soon churned the sea to a white frenzy and we realised we'd have to wait another day, rationing the wine, fruit, cheese and a half loaf of bread.

That night, sitting before the fire, eating our meagre fare, Walt and I, avoiding the eyes of the children, made up lame stories about what fun it was to be castaways. If the sounds of the previous night had been awesome, those of the second night were positively terrifying. The heavings, sighings, groanings and creakings were magnified many times over, now accompanied by torrential rain that beat upon the metal roof adding to the din.

Nor did daybreak bring any relief from the ferocity of the gale. Walt and the boys alternated between trying to find some dry wood and securing the boat as she bounced and thumped against the jetty. The storm raged for three days and our food dwindled to an alarmingly low level. Thankfully, the fourth day brought clearing skies; the sea subsided and in due course the punt rumbled on to the beach. Our worldly possessions were carried lovingly to the house with the fond hope that their presence would make it a home.

The first few days at Aotea could hardly be described as idyllic. Rather they were a blur of screaming winds, leaking roof, mud, wet clothing and hunger pangs. Little Bertha did nothing to alleviate our problems, for when we tried to approach her for warmth or food, she issued forth tongues of acrid smoke from every aperture she could find. Feeding her on a diet of wet wood did nothing to improve her disposition.

Eventually a routine of sorts was established and our life at Aotea began in earnest. Mornings started with cajoling Bertha into action, a procedure she always objected to. Breakfast, then Roy and Mary settled into Correspondence Schooling and, while Walt and Mitch made off to the job of the day, I headed for the creek, trying to clear it of tins, beer bottles and sludge.

As I worked, strange, lizard-like creatures sat unblinking along the banks watching my labours, darting under rocks if they caught me watching them. Even stranger creatures came up from the depths of the creek — fish without eyes and quite transparent, possessing the amazing ability to live in the muck and mire. They flapped and wriggled in my hands as I carried them downstream, hoping they would survive.

I froze in my tracks when I saw a large, ugly insect crawling up the leg of my trousers as I sat resting on a log. Jumping to my feet, I screamed in terror and tried to shake it off, but it held on and refused to be dislodged. When I grabbed a stick and pried at its hold, it did a most peculiar thing — it gave the clenched fist salute of the black people, or at least a good imitation of it. My screams brought Walt running and he bravely lifted the creepy crawler from my leg and deposited it on the ground. This was my first encounter with a weta and, although I've long passed the screaming stage, they still give me a prickly chill.

Walt sawed, hammered and swore with precise regularity as he added to and subtracted from the little grey house, arranging it to suit our needs and after several weeks of steady work, we had managed to make the place quite livable. Roy and Mitch made a double-sized bunk bed using four trees for the corner posts and smaller ones for the ladder, giving them each a full-size bed, a creation that would prove to be a topic of conversation for years to come.

A garden site was selected and digging commenced. What should have taken three days took nearly four weeks. The hard clay and thick cutty grass refused to yield to shovel or hoe. Digging became a full-time occupation for the men, accompanied by the persistent odour of Deep Heat rubbed into young and aging muscles alike as the next step to self-sufficiency slowly became a receptacle for the numerous seedlings and seeds we had accumulated. All were sown with tender, loving care and we fed them on various concoctions of garlic, Maxicrop and fish skeletons while we waited for the first official shovel of magic earth from our newly established compost bin.

Our efforts were completely devastated by the southerly wind that crept across the surrounding hills and with one frigid blast reduced the seedlings to dust. We planted again and waited. Dutifully, the shoots appeared, reaching a bare six centimetres, only to be devoured by a wild, long-horned steer that munched contentedly through the garden one night as we slept. What he missed with his mouth, he smashed with his feet, leaving nothing untouched in his wake.

Old Man Southerly returned to play havoc with the third and fourth attempts; obviously something had to be done. Mitch erected a wire fence and poked it full of manuka branches. In theory, it was to act as windbreak and steer-deterrent. In practice, it did neither. The steer found it useful to rub his tough hide against and the next southerly flattened it like so many matchsticks.

In his own fashion, Walt solved the problem. After several sleepless nights he announced, 'We'll build a greenhouse that will act as a windbreak'.

Permit in hand, the men designed and built a large structure directly in the path of the prevailing wind. The roof was angled to deflect the wind up and over not only the existing garden, but the terraced extensions now creeping up the hill on the other side of the creek. To hold these terraces in place, we built three stone walls, each about 23 metres long and over a metre high. Initially, each stone had been brought half a kilometre by wheelbarrow, until someone came up with the idea of a flying fox. Roy and Mitch scrambled through the scrub, dragging a piece of heavy-duty wire and searching for a suitable place to secure it on the hill above the homestead. A sizable cabbage tree was selected and the wire strung from the tree to the top shed. Next, a pulley was fastened to the wire and from it hung a large basket which, when full of rocks, was to be set free to slide to those of us waiting at the shed. At least, that was the way we planned it.

Climbing to the top of the cabbage tree, Roy launched the basket on its maiden voyage. It slid slowly at first, catching on the wire, then, bouncing and weaving, it began the descent over treetops and homestead, gaining momentum as it raced towards us. By the time it passed over the garden, it had enough speed on to have been launched from the Kennedy space pad and I wondered who was going to catch it. As the stone-filled meteor bore down, only one course of action seemed expedient and, just in time, Walt and I dived in separate directions to avoid the crashing onslaught. It roared past us and smashed into the wall of the top shed, leaving a gaping hole.

'How'd it go?' yelled the boys from the hill.

Picking ourselves up from the dust and surveying the shed, we

Samantha and her latest set of twins. She was the only Arapawa doe that gave birth to triplets. All three of the little does survived, but here she takes Samson and his sister for a walk in the hills

Saba, one of the twins born to Samantha when Marcia and Rachael first came to Aotea. The distinctive markings on Saba show the Arapawa markings that distinguish the bucks. Sometimes this 'Jerusalem Cross' becomes a full shoulder marking dark and resplendent.

Our "Dream House", Richboro, Pennsylvania, U.S.A. Nestled in two acres of woodland and fitted with every conceivable mod-con. We left it in search of another and different sort of a dream.

called the boys home for a conference on our procedures.

The second attempt was improved by adding a rope to control the speed of the basket and it seemed to work until the momentum became too great for Roy to feed out the rope at an appropriate pace. Consequently, the basket tipped, showering rocks on the homestead roof, the greenhouse and the garden and causing unbearable tension on Roy's hands. He was forced to let go and once more Walt and I had to dive for cover as the basket hurtled past us and through the hole in the shed wall, where it deposited the second basket of rocks. As a method of transporting rocks from point A to B, it filled the bill, but, balanced against repairing the shed, homestead, greenhouse and garden, it left much to be desired. We abandoned our modern invention in favour of the lowly wheelbarrow.

Mitch became the prime force behind the 'Green Thumb Brigade', spending hours reading and experimenting with organic methods of growing our food. Compost, a new word for us, became the order of the day, and everything that had once been alive was put into a bin to return magically as healthy, black soil which we applied lavishly to the garden, replacing the hard clay.

We leapt about the garden, chasing white butterflies with a fly swatter. Slugs and slaters were hand-piced from the plants and aphids were ruthlessly drowned in soapy water, for no sprays or chemicals were to touch our garden of Eden. Some things flourished while others were munched mercilessly by invading insects, but as the compost-rich soil improved, so did the health of the plants, and the insects lost interest. In time, the fly swatter became redundant and the garden burst forth to meet our greatest expectations.

Our next venture was into the poultry arena and on a trip to the mainland, we collected 12 hens and a rooster for $28. We installed them in a nice new henhouse and dreamed of omelettes. Unfortunately our birds turned out to be rather ancient and the only one that knew its function was the rooster who woke us at 3.30 each morning, while the old girls poked around for worms and grubs and never looked at the nests. I was bemoaning our eggless hens to a visitor one day and was told we should have purchased 'perching pullets'. So we procured some young birds just bursting to lay and they did — everywhere but in the furnished nests. Collecting the eggs became a challenge. One little black hen thought she was a stork and laid high in a tree ensuring I got my daily exercise as I teetered and grunted my way to and from her nest each evening. A randy rooster with 24 ladies-in-waiting did nothing for my planned parenthood scheme and before long, many a lady came home followed by several cheeping balls of fluff.

One of our major efforts, and undoubtedly our worst mistake, was the installation of an 11-kilowatt generator. Our ideas about the rough and ready life were still greatly tempered by our years in the consumer society and we felt certain things would be necessary for us to survive and they required power.

A hole was dug, cement poured and a shed erected to house the generator which, in our folly, we located a mere 20 metres from the house. Supreme effort was required to get the 11-kilowatt Goliath from punt to shed. Once it was in place we had only to await the arrival of the electricians and we'd have lights, power tools, freezer and fridge; no more prowling about after dark with kerosene lanterns or sawing every piece of wood by hand. With a freezer we wouldn't have to eat a whole sheep in fast order and we could save some of the garden's bounty for lean winter months. As it was, we had a very unbalanced diet, although an organic one. We ate like Henry the Eighth three times a day or were rationed to potatoes and more potatoes when the garden was dormant. Somehow, we'd missed the page in the *Mother Earth Almanac* that said not to plant all the peas or carrots at once and had grown ourselves into a feast or famine syndrome. The first attempts at preserving meat in brine produced a nauseating concoction which even the dogs refused to eat and the chickens eyed with suspicion. The generator and all its accessories would be a great boon to Aotea.

It was during one of those 'potatoes or nothing' gaps in our garden production that the electricians arrived quite out of the blue for we hadn't expected them until after Christmas.

The day had started out normally enough with the men off mustering, Mary doing correspondence and I attending to chores. When I went to the jetty to meet the mailboat, a young man leaned over the side and asked, 'Are you expecting visitors?'

'No,' I replied. 'Not really.'

'Well,' he smiled cheerily as he swung on to the jetty, 'you've got 'em.' And with that, he and another man began unloading copious amounts of wire, boxes, tools and coil. It had begun raining and everything had to be carted hastily into the woolshed. While we trotted back and forth like worker ants, I felt something akin to panic. I had not ordered any extra groceries and the next boat was four days away.

'The others will be here later today,' announced my cheery friend.

'Others?' I squeaked.

'Yep, and we'll a place to bunk down for a couple of days.'

Fortunately, Mary and I had made a pot of potato soup that morning that they heartily enjoyed, to the last drop. Then they proceeded to turn the house into an uproar as we were 'wired in'. Tools, dust, drills and yards of wire trailed from room to room, out windows and through doors. The animals soon discovered these places of admittance and we quickly had an assortment of dogs, chickens and lambs romping through.

I was frantically searching my cookbooks for ideas on preparing potatoes to feed nine people for three days when I looked up to see our boat pulling into the jetty. Running through the open door to tell Walt that he'd have to make a trip to town for food, I saw he was being supported by the boys and his T-shirt was covered with blood. A huge gash ran along his jawbone and the flesh lay open in an angry wound that seemed to run from ear to ear.

We managed to find a place in lie him amidst the pandemonium and to wash the blood from his face. He had, the boys told me, fallen over a cliff on to the rocks below.

The wound definitely needed stitches, but Walt would not hear of a trip to town with all else that was going on. We made up some butterfly adhesives and, while the boys held the wound together, I secured it in about six places, then gave him some red wine to replace the lost blood; why I don't know, it just seemed the thing to do.

Meanwhile, the 'others' had arrived, adding to the confusion. Mary and I were in the process of making potato patties for a late lunch when Walt's leg went into spasm and we dropped everything and ran for the 'Natural Healing' book which was all we had in the way of first aid.

'What are you going to do for him?' asked a concerned electrician.

'I'm wrapping his leg in cabbage compresses.'

'Cabbage!' he repeated incredulously as I dashed past him with buckets of steaming cabbage and proceeded to encase Walt's leg from ankle to thigh in steamed greens, securing them with a string. The four men looked hesitantly at each other, perhaps wondering if this was the safest place to spend the night.

Walt sat propped up in bed, a picture of abject misery, blood-stained, bits of adhesive stuck to his chin, one leg green and steaming and sipping a glass of wine. I sat with him for a while, pondering if this was what was meant by getting away from it all and wondering if those precious cabbage leaves could be recycled if our food ran out.

We tried lunch again, only to have our attempts aborted as Walt cried out in pain. Dashing to the bedroom, we found him hopping around on one leg, the other held stiffly out in front of him as he grasped his tortured thigh with his hand, thereby securing a fistful of soggy cabbage. All the yelling and hopping had broken open the butterflies and blood was spurting everywhere. Guiding Walt to the bathroom through a maze of men, wires and assorted chickens, we tried the 'healing with water' method, spraying his leg with hot water for one minute, followed by cold, alternating until the spasm stopped. The bathroom floor and those of us dealing with Walt were covered in an unbelievable mixture of blood, water and cabbage and I was in no condition to answer the queries of the electricians as to where I preferred my hot points and power outlets as I shooed chickens, chased lambs, swore at Bertha and tried to mop up the mess.

Lunch was served to the bewildered workers at 4.30 p.m. The next few hours were spent holding Walt's chin together, wrapping his leg in cabbage ans spraying him with hot and cold water until relief finally came. I alternated between potatoes souffled and au gratin, green poultices and trying to concentrate on hot points. Walt eventually fell asleep through a combination of pain, fatigue and plasma in the form of red wine. Dinner was served at 10.30 p.m. with Mary and I doing the dishes at midnight by lantern light.

Walt awoke feeling terrible, but at least the spasms had stopped and his chin was holding together. Most of his discomfort was the result of a huge hangover and he remained in bed holding his head, chin and leg, the head being given priority as the electricians drilled and banged.

It was sheer madness for several days. I endeavoured to produce meals on wheels for Walt and feed us all on the humble potato. The boys stoked Bertha to capacity and she puffed and billowed in rage at the extra demands made upon her for we required copious amounts of hot water for cooking, cleaning and bathing our temporary family of nine. Mary laid siege to the kitchen and baked valiantly to fill the gaps in our diet.

In due course, we were finally 'wired in' and it was time to test the generators. We were advised to turn on all electrical appliances and pulled out our four heaters from Southland, the iron, toaster, and so on. The interior of the house soon had the temperature of a sauna, aided and abetted by Bertha chugging away at top speed and, as we laboured in the kitchen, blinking away the perspiration that trickled into our eyes, Mary and I became increasingly comatose.

Heat stroke was prevented by frequent dashes to the beach where we lowered ourselves into the water and sizzled like two fried sausages.

On one of my trips through the lounge, I collapsed in a chair for a moment's respite, drew in a deep breath and smelt smoke! Visions of faulty wiring, perhaps clogged with cabbage leaves, crossed my mind and the dreaded thought that we might have to start again had us all, electricians included, frantically searching the house for the problem. Everything appeared to be in order, yet the smell of burning wood persisted and it was only when we lifted the toaster from the floor where it had been placed to add to the load, that we found the source of the trouble — the floorboards lay smouldering and black beneath.

The greatest shock came when the 'genny' was turned on. Its thunder and thumping so close to the house drove us mad. Suddenly the many uses planned for its power seemed unimportant in comparison with having our peace and quiet shattered. The first step in reversing the consequences of our mistake was to trade in the electric fridge-freezer for a kerosene one. This still left me with mountains of mutton, but peace and quiet meant more than convenience.

News of our escapades at Aotea somehow reached the outside world and more and more visitors began arriving, some out of curiosity about the Yanks living in the Sounds; others to welcome and encourage and assist where possible. Many became dear friends and everyone was generous and kind.

Some days left us with no time for anything but entertaining. We'd often find ourselves saying farewell to a boatload of people on one side of the jetty, then turning to welcome another. Wining and dining became a full-time occupation and we met a variety of people; it was interesting, exhilarating, fun and exhausting.

The 'Top of the South' folk were as generous as their Southland counterparts and we received gifts of fruit trees, ducks, saw benches, clothes, books, as well as help and advice. And we also received two piglets no bigger than a three-week-old puppy. 'Just the thing,' said the hearty donors. 'Raise yourselves a bit of pork.'

It was a thoughtful gesture, but we knew nothing about pigs and received our two new steps to self-sufficiency with something less than confidence. With a mixed bag of advice that ranged from 'You'll never raise them' to 'Pigs are easy to raise', I embarked upon the time-consuming task of being surrogate mother to two tiny creatures that screamed when touched and bit me each time I tried to feed them.

I carted pans of warm soggy food which they insisted upon wading through or tipping over with their probing noses which, in turn, meant removing them from their kennel to change the bedding. Their shrieks created hysteria among the dogs, who would come rushing on to the scene, lunging and snapping at the piglets who screamed louder and bit harder while I tried to restore order.

It took many days and countless Band Aids before I had convinced them that food was for eating and I was their friend. This truce established, they became insatiable, their appetites knowing no bounds. They lost all traces of their former antagonism and, once released from their pen, insisted on following me everywhere, including into the house. I relented and allowed them in on a few occasions, only to regret it each time, for they wrecked havoc.

As they grew to the size of large dogs, it became a feat of dexterity to beat two very determined pigs through the door. On more than one occasion, I had to resort to trickery by pretending to head for the front door, then rushing quickly to the back before they realised what had happened. This was followed by great displays of indignation, demonstrated by their bashing at the door, squealing and standing on their hind legs and rubbing their great muddy noses across the newly-installed ranch-sliders.

Another of their favourite pastimes was to nose through the wash as I pegged it out, select a choice piece and run off with it, while I followed in hot pursuit. Usually we ended up with a tug-of-war and several pieces of torn clothing.

I was beginning to get decidedly impatient looks from the family and the pair did nothing to enhance their popularity by ploughing up the front lawn into ruts and ridges that turned the pathway to the house into a quagmire with each rain. Holding a telephone conversation became impossible, for as soon as they heard my voice (unfortunately the phone was by the back door) they created such a commotion I could hear nothing and the person on the other end was left to wonder what all the screaming was about! I tried to alleviate the problem by feeding them while talking and kept a supply of dog biscuits, bread and barley handy. By juggling the phone between ear and shoulder, I managed to hold the door and toss food to them for the duration of the conversation. In time, they became complete extortionists and I felt sure they knew which ring on the party line was ours, for they seemed to be at the back door before I could say 'Hello'.

By now, we knew Grunt and Snort would never become pork chops or bacon, but their presence was causing dissension and I couldn't see them improving with age. They were now as big as Labradors, loving and pugnacious, possessing a devilish sense of humour and an unerring aptitude for getting into trouble; qualities that were both infuriating and forgivable. However, in an attempt to keep marital stability, it was agreed the pigs must go . . . away from the house. They were released into one of the paddocks far from the homestead, where to our great relief, they stayed for many months.

One day, when I went to let the dogs off for a run, I spied a great black nose protruding from a large clump of grass and I approached cautiously. The nose sniffed, then rose, followed by three tiny noses. Grunt's huge black hulk came rushing forward nearly knocking me over as she rubbed against my legs and leaned heavily against me to show her affection. The three little ones stayed in the nest while Grunt and I had a great rubbing and hugging session. Then, reassured, the piglets came timidly to us. Grunt was as proud as any mother and positively glowed when I praised her for being so clever.

Grunt and her trio were soon joined by Snort and we had five bulldozers happily ploughing up the front lawn. Needless to say, Walt was not overjoyed and pointed to the ominous-looking tusks which Snort had developed during his parental fling.

The dogs, now aware of the pigs' superior size and strength, had long since ceased reacting to each squeal and had come to accept the pigs as part of the establishment. In fact, Tipua, Mitch's sheepdog, had allowed her four pups to become friends with Grunt's piglets and the seven little black babies had a wonderful time chasing and wrestling and they provided us with hours of enjoyment. One day I was watching them from the kitchen window and saw the piglets indicate to Grunt their need for a drink, whereby she obligingly flopped down on one side exposing a long row of swollen teats. The puppies, watching the piglets suckling noisily and greedily, decided their comradeship should extend beyond the fun and frolic, so they ambled over to where Grunt lay and latched on to four more of her teats, vying with the piglets for better positions. I had not expected Grunt to tolerate this breach of protocol, but to my surprise and delight, she never moved and let the puppies suckle their fill.

Sadly, Snort had to be destroyed when he became a rather too playful and restless boar and a menace to the numerous visitors to Aotea. The alternative was to keep him penned, which I could not do. Even sadder was the loss of Grunt, caused by a severe case of mastitis after her second litter. But the friendship and trust of these two intelligent rascals is still remembered.

So the first few years at Aotea rolled by swiftly, full of surprises, fun, heartache and disappointment — joy and laughter, all mingled together. One thing was clear — life was neither dull nor predictable. One day could be perfect bliss, the next — a disaster. But, above all, we had become aware of three major factors that shaped our lives. They were the land, the sea and 'Old Man Southerly'.

The land had received us graciously, despite our ineptitude and mistakes; our garden flourished and abounded with growing things of all descriptions, giving us more than we needed and providing us with some to share with friends.

The sea, which we had in the past admired from the safety of the land, had soon taught us to listen more carefully to her song, for from tranquil repose, she can erupt into instant fury, untamed and merciless.

On a return trip from town one day, she caught us unaware, clawing at our boat with icy fingers and tossing us about like leaves in a storm. I sat on the floor of the boat, holding on for dear life and frightened out of my wits. The boys were with me and Roy was struggling to keep the boat on course. From my seat on the floor, I looked up to walls of water above me as we leaned heavily to one side. Then the horizon tilted crazily, the boat falling into the trough of the passing wave. As the senior member of this expedition, I tried to remain calm, rather hard to do when you feel you might drown at any minute, but watching Roy's battle at the wheel, I didn't want to lessen his confidence by putting on a life-jacket.

The sea came at us from all directions, one moment threatening to swallow us completely, then thrusting us high on the crest of the wave, leaving us without power or steering. Water poured over the sides, the stern and the bow, drenching us to the skin. Great fountains of water, whipped by the wind, slammed into the boat sending us side-on to the approaching swell. Mitch braced himself in the cabin door and finally, too frightened for pretended bravery, I clutched his leg and hung on. Roy managed to get the boat running with the sea and we then took off at an amazing speed and surfed into the bay and safety. Walt grabbed the ropes thrown to him as we hurtled past the jetty and we stepped ashore after four hours of harrowing battle.

The 'Old Man Southerly' is the third part of the trinity. Frigid winds gather from the south, lift above the hills around us and roar with unbelievable ferocity across the bay. One tenses with the approaching rumble which resembles a runaway freight train and, with closed eyes, waits for the impact. Sometimes the wind crackles and snaps as it whips through the high grass on the hills, leaving echoes like the sound of rifles being fired. Accompanied by rain, the Old Man whips, stings and beats all into submission, inspiring awe and sometimes fear. He has turned several boats upside down on our mooring and sent a large dinghy hurtling through space on to our front lawn, almost decapitating Mitch as he walked to the house. Trees bow deeply to him as he passes, then snap to attention, limbs dangling and broken. We have been swept off our feet as we met him coming around a bend in the track and, on one very bad night, he knocked the chimney off the roof.

There were other forces, less obvious in their influence, yet subtly moulding our thoughts and actions and stripping us of a lifelong veneer. 'Getting away from it all' took us on divergent paths.

Some in the family found it beneficial to be alone, others were lonely. Peace and quiet meant boredom for the children and communing with nature had its antithesis in repairing the damage 'Old Man Southerly' caused in his latest rip through Aotea. The pride in self-sufficiency was often drowned by sacrifice, denial of comfort and a longing for the good old days of immediate gratification when every need had not to be preceded by hours of muscle-racking work.

We could not be, and indeed realised we no longer needed to be, all things to each other. We had clung together knowing no other way to survive, but Aotea, the school of hard knocks, had taught us individual resiliency, a kind of interdependence based on independence. Consensus of opinion fragmented and, while survival was paramount, we no longer felt compelled to pull together like horses in harness.

My own journey into unchartered waters began when three infant animals were brought home to Aotea, although at the time I never dreamed their presence would cause such disruption. The three little animals that changed my life were two Arapawa goats and a wild Arapawa lamb. As with Grunt and Snort, I set about being mother to the orphans and learning more of the ways of those I wrongly assumed to have been born free.

I named the baby goats Samantha and Jody. Jody had been the victim of a shooter who had killed her mother and left the baby wounded, her front leg a weeping, festering sore where the bullet had penetrated, shattering the bone. Walt found her huddled next to the stiff, hardened carcass of her mother where she had still instinctively sought food and security. She must have been there a long time for she was emaciated and ill when Walt brought her home and I felt she would surely die. Samantha, on the other hand, was robust, vocal, independent and scornful of any attempt to tame her wild spirit and was to remain forever so. The wild lamb was shy, with bright brown eyes that followed us cautiously. Her shaggy covering of wool was the colour of rust and she amazed me with her lack of fear and her dignity.

Most of my attention was given to Jody who needed constant care. I treated her leg with a mixture of Vaseline and kelp, bathing it first in warm sea water and changing the dressing four times a day. We dared not allow her more than a few ounces of milk at a time, lest her shrunken stomach rebel, so we fed her every two hours, hardening ourselves to her plaintive cries for more. Sam, by contrast, was very much in charge of the situation. From the start, she refused to take a bottle and no amount of persuasion could change her mind. I'd get her on the floor, my knees resting on the ground as I straddled her back and tried to force open her clenched jaws. If I did manage to force the teat into her mouth, she refused to suck, clamping her little mouth around the teat in a vice-like grip and glaring up at me in defiance as the milk dripped on to the floor.

Once her initial cravings were satisfied, Jody posed no problem and was content to lie snuggled in the straw-filled box next to Bertha. Samantha was like a jack-in-the-box, popping out faster than I could return her to the high-sided container prepared for her comfort. Having escaped, she charged about the kitchen doing battle with all and sundry. This minute creature was possessed of such unshakable nerve that she won my instant admiration. She made it clear she didn't want or need my maternal outpourings, but would tolerate me as she had no place else to go. She would come and sit by me if she so chose, but I could never cuddle her and make soft murmuring sounds as I did with Jody who would fall contentedly asleep in my arms. My kitchen was Sam's playground and anything she could reach, her toys; consequently things were in disarray until Jody recovered and the goats were evicted to the chicken house.

Sam immediately asserted her authority over the poultry and made it clear the henhouse was now her home, the result being that some of the hens took to the trees to sleep. Sam eventually discovered the garden, which, being Sam, she assumed we had grown for her consumption. It was at this point she met some formidable opposition in the person of Mitch who under no circumstances was about to relinquish his kingdom to this four-legged liberated female and both went to great lengths in efforts to outwit each other. I got the impression Sam was winning, for it became commonplace to hear Mitch's roar of impatience: 'Mom, Samantha's in the garden . . . AGAIN!' This was the signal for a quick exit and Sam would head for the fence, grabbing mouthfuls and managing to keep a safe distance between herself and Mitch before squeezing through the wire and romping off to safety, leaving me to reap the verbal abuse from an understandably annoyed son. We tried putting a wooden triangle around her neck, an obstruction that would foil any goat's attempts at fence-crashing, but Sam figured it out in half a day and by a few extra manoeuvres wriggled in and out of the garden as much as she had before.

My experiences with Grunt and Snort, plus the obvious independence of Samantha, should have taught me that my services as surrogate mother were appreciated in some ways and totally useless in others, but somehow I believed I'd have to teach Jody and Sam the art of climbing as they had no mothers to pass on the mysteries of nature. Off we went, Sam frisking and frolicking, Jody, limping only slightly, walking quietly by my side. We ambled along one of the numerous tracks etched into the hillsides by countless generations of sheep, wild goats and pigs and headed for the wilder and more remote reaches of Aotea until I found a suitably steep cliff. It looked a perfect training ground for my charges and we began the first lesson.

They managed to keep pace with me, which I thought encouraging, and I ventured ever higher, calling to them to follow. Oblivious to the danger, I climbed and called. Near to the summit, I turned to see how the goats were faring and was struck with a terrifying case of vertigo. Afraid to move in any direction, I clung by my fingertips and toes, head swimming and heart pounding, feeling my stomach knot in cold fear. Samantha leapt to a ledge above me and looked down on my predicament with apparent amusement, showering me with pebbles and bits of earth. No-one knew where I had gone and would have no idea in which direction to search. I probably wouldn't be missed until dinner time when hungry stomachs guided the men to the house.

It was now 2.30 in the afternoon and, vertigo or not, I realised that hanging there until six was out of the question. 'It is, Elizabeth, a matter of conquering your fear and just moving slowly down the cliff. Even if someone was here, you'd still have to climb down.' So I muttered to myself as I searched for a foothold below, that lump of fear still heavy in my belly. It took several hours to inch my way to ground level, the last two metres covered in record time as I lost my footing and tumbled the remaining distance almost as fast as the goats did. Sam had long since tired of the outing and had skimmed past and out of sight. Jody stayed with me for moral support and together we limped home where we were greeted by Sam lying on the front step. Thus I learned one does not teach goats to climb. They have a built in agility and derring-do that needs no assistance from mere mortals.

Geep, the wild lamb, so named when we were advised by locals she was half-goat and half-sheep, had found a friend in Cassidy, a pet ewe, and fortunately required little attention. Cassidy had been raised with Sam and Jody and acquired many caprine habits. To see this large, heavy ewe aspiring to the twirls and pirouettes of the goats reminded me of the hippos in Walt Disney's *Fantasia*, adorned in mini-skirts and attempting a delicate ballet. Even when Cassidy became a sedate old lady, she still persisted with capricious behaviour.

Fortunately, Geep remained convinced she was a sheep, albeit a very black one. In addition to her knowing brown eyes and rusty black wool, she came complete with a white topknot and a tail of equal parts, black and white. Her name suggested our initial doubts as to her ancestry, but further inquiries only produced more confusion with an array of answers and theories. I decided to try to solve the mystery myself. The Auckland Zoo politely replied that they had no knowledge of the sheep and referred me to the Ruakura Research Station, who tersely informed me this was hardly within their realm of interest and referred me to Massey University who referred me to no-one — they didn't bother to reply. Mr Bell from Wildlife Services responded with assurances that their interest in feral sheep was usually directed towards exterminating them and he referred me to the D.S.I.R.

Fortunately, or so I thought, the buck had only one more pass to make and that was to the Ecology Division, where finally my photographs of the wild sheep came to rest and a spark of interest was generated. The wild sheep, which had roamed the hills of Arapawa for over a century, now became the subject of intense study. They were measured, weighed, examined and photographed from all angles and declared to be of scientific and historic value.

Geep was joined by several more ewes and a rather ancient ram with the hopes of keeping the breed alive, although just what breed they represented was still unknown, despite the flurry of scientific activity. We were proud to have played a part in the subsequent preservation of the sheep, even though our involvement meant time spent away from the farm and a trip through the never-never land of bureaucracy.

The diversion caused by my interest in the wild sheep should have served as a warning signal; if you want to get away from it all, whatever you do, don't get involved! From then on, any hopes of living the quiet, secluded life was left behind, to resurface only in daydreams and rare moments of reflection on what might have been.

For the escapist, it is best to know nothing, observe nothing, read nothing, hear nothing and above all, say nothing. Involvement can mean commitment, and commitment calls for a measure of determination. Add these ingredients to female stubbornness, put everything in a pot and stir; the result is most definitely not a recipe for remaining anonymous.

So while Walt and I spun through the days of new adventure and challenge we were too occupied to notice the growing restlessness in the children. Only slowly did we realise that they were less than satisfied with our isolation and our spartan way of life and were, in fact, growing up with ideas and aspirations of their own.

They had been young when we left the States — Mitch 15, Mary 14 and Roy 12. With good grace and trust they had accepted all the new experiences our decision to leave had thrust upon them, adjusting to a totally new schooling system where uniforms were the order of the day and students sprang to attention when the headmaster entered a room. There had been new friends to make and old ones to try to forget, not easy in the heady, emotional yars of adolescence. Mitch had assumed the man's role when Walt was in hospital and had been called upon to kill a sheep for the dogs in Walt's absence, a deed that might come easy for a youth raised on a farm but was definitely traumatic for an urban lad.

His classmates had elected him head prefect, which attested to their respect for and acceptance of him. After sitting his final exams, he had found a job with the tourist bureau, rented a caravan, bought an old jalopy and moved towards independence. It had taken more than friendly persuasion to convince him to leave Te Anau and come with us, forfeiting his new-found freedom.

Mary had experienced the first sparks of romance in Te Anau as the fresh-faced youths vied for a date with the pretty Yankee lass. Aotea had little to offer a girl who enjoyed being a girl and was certainly devoid of fresh-faced youths, as most of our visitors were adults. Consequently, she seldom saw anyone of her own age. But it was Mary who stood by me as we coped with the rising tide of people, performing miracles on Little Bertha. When I'd feel the panic rise, it was Mary's calm assurance that saved the day. She coined one of our favourite expressions on the day we sweltered with Bertha and the heaters to feed the electricians. As I rushed around, bemoaning the potato's lack of versatility and my own fate, Mary plodded on and, putting her arm around me, said 'Not to worry, Mom'.

Roy had accepted our new life with the same vigour and enthusiasm he had brought to the old. A mere shift of 10,000 miles did nothing to dampen his happy-go-lucky nature. He was the first to go roaming in Te Anau, finding new friends, old and young alike. He had managed to get himself an after-school job with a fencing contractor and also had managed to fall over a roll of barbed wire leaving him with a wound that required 15 stitches. It was Roy's knowledge of fencing that helped Walt over the one rough spot in Pelorus Sound when he was called upon to erect a fence.

Thus the children had followed us as we followed our dream. But the time was approaching for them to dream their own dreams, follow their own hearts and, as fledglings from a nest, begin to fly.

CHAPTER V

Changing Winds

'Dad's just vaccinated himself for pulpy kidney and blackleg,' Roy remarked as he poured himself a cup of tea. As an afterthought he added, 'Oh, yeah, and Janet fell in the dip too.'

'Who did what?' I exclaimed.

Reviewing the events, Roy informed me that our niece, who had arrived from the States only the day before, had indeed fallen into the sheep dip. She had asked if she could help and was assigned the job of pushing the sheep under with a broad-based piece of wood as they swam past. It isn't the easiest task, but the alternative involves wrestling with fully grown ewes that are, at best, reluctant to enter the bath and have to be individually manhandled or unceremoniously pushed.

Jan positioned herself, leaning out over the dip and waited, plunger poised, only to miss as the first ewe paddled past, her lunge for the sheep's head propelling her into the murky water where she promptly sank to the bottom.

Walt, meanwhile, endeavouring to inoculate an uncooperative ewe against such nasties as pulpy kidney and blackleg, had lost his hold on the old girl at the moment of contact and had injected his thumb instead.

'Well, don't just stand there, do something!' I snapped, heading for the yards, wondering why everything happened at once. One catastrophe wasn't enough, we always had to hit the double-banger. Mitch had hauled Janet from the dip and resubmerged her in the sea, dunking her up and down like a doughnut in a cup of coffee, hoping to wash away as much of the poison as possible. Janet's fall had exposed her to the chemical added to the water for the control of lice on the sheep and while it had no adverse effect on the sheep, we had no way of knowing what it might do to Jan. She stood on the beach, bedraggled, sodden and smelling strongly of lice control and Walt sat holding his thumb, casting menacing looks at the ewe.

I decided Janet was the one who needed attention first. While Walt's kidneys might be churning to a pulp and his feet turning black, it was possible that Janet was in grave danger. I rushed her to the shower and scrubbed until she was raw, but, despite copious amounts of soap and shampoo, she was still emitting a powerful aroma and I was becoming thoroughly alarmed.

While she was changing her clothes, I rang the doctor and, in hushed tones lest Jan hear me, explained what had happened and our mounting fears for her. The advice from the doctor was to ring the vet where the chemical had been purchased and find out just what substance we were dealing with. It was, the vet informed me, a chemical that is absorbed through the skin and the wisest course was to ring the Poison Centre in Dunedin.

The Poison Centre assured me we had done the right things so far, but now Jan must be kept under observation for 24 hours and, under no circumstances should she be allowed to fall asleep in the next few hours. If she showed any signs of drowsiness or nausea, I should ring immediately. They would keep a helicopter standing by.

None of this was very reassuring and, when Jan emerged from the bedroom with a blanket and announced she was going out on the lawn for a rest, I almost collapsed. She was, she said, feeling fine, but all the dipping and dunking, plus a case of jetlag had made her weary; she just wanted to rest.

The last words of advice from the Poison Centre had been not to let Janet suspect she might be poisoned as she could, through anxiety, present the symptoms. Trying to appear casual, I followed her to the lawn where she spread her blanket and lay down with a contented sign and closed her eyes, hoping, no doubt, I'd take the hint and leave her to recover from her initiation to Aotea. This I could not do and I launched into a talkathon that would have made any filibuster envious. Janet yawned, blinked and stared hollow-eyed at the torrent of words as I covered every subject from the one-celled amoeba to Greek mythology in an effort to keep her awake.

' "To be or not to be, that is the question," ' I recited.

Janet blinked.

' "Whether 'tis nobler in the mind to suffer the slings and arrows of outrageous fortune" ', wondering how you could tell the difference between jetlag drowsiness and just plain drowsiness.

' "Or to take arms against a sea of troubles, and by opposing, end them".'

Janet yawned.

I stopped short, for the next line mentioned sleep and Janet was nearly there without the help of Shakespeare.

'Janet,' I asked brightly, 'do you know what Hamlet meant by a

Angela, a friend staying at Aotea cuddles Katy, while Daffodil looks on. Katy and Daffy were but two of the many orphaned Arapawa goats I raised and which helped form the basis of the surviving herd at Aotea.

Sue Grant taking notes for an article in the New Zealand Deerstalkers' magazine Wild Life. The sportsmen of New Zealand have always received my message of conservation with understanding and support.

When I was covered in salt water and sand and bone tired after a day of mustering the goats, the press sought an interview. This photo has appeared many times with various articles and stories about the Arapawa wildlife.

"bare bodkin"?'

'Not really,' she replied, rubbing her eyes. 'Who cares, anyway?'

'Well, as far as I can make out, a bodkin is a dagger.'

'Uh huh,' whispered Janet, her eyes at half-mast.

'Oh God, how am I going to keep her awake,' I moaned to myself. Short of dowsing her with cold water, physically shaking her into awareness or blasting her with a loud version of the 1812 Overture, which might make her suspicious, there seemed no way to induce her to remain awake without being more obvious than I'd already been.

Remembering Walt's unhappy thumb, I reluctantly left Janet for the moment and headed for the house to consult the vet book. If Walt had succeeded in giving himself a mild case of pulpy kidney, these were the symptoms to watch for — abdominal pain, bleating, mild scour (with head thrown back), paddling of legs and champing of jaws. Blackleg, on the other hand, caused depression, unwillingness to eat, the wool would pluck easily and there might be lameness.

I pointed to Walt that over the years he had displayed one or more of these symptoms to a varying degree without the benefit of an inoculation and differentiating between a reaction to the injection he had given himself and the fact that he was just having a bad day might be difficult.

His throbbing thumb and disgruntled disposition prevented his appreciating the humour of my diagnosis and, telling the kids to watch him for signs of bleating or champing, I hurried back to Janet. I fabricated some reason or other for disturbing her and spent the rest of the day keeping her so occupied, physically and verbally, that she had no chance to get near a bed. Her peculiar looks in my direction indicated she thought I was behaving strangely and I hoped she would put it down to old age or too much smog-free air.

Pulling a few hairs from the beginnings of Walt's Friar Tuck patch on the back of his head and noting the ease with which they parted company, I teasingly announced the first symptoms of blackleg: the wool plucks easily. By reminding him of the time he had been carried home to be encased in cabbage leaves and suggesting that the spasms he endured were not unlike legs a-paddling, we cajoled him back into good humour.

Fortunately, Walt's only legacy from the inoculation was a very sore thumb and throughout the rest of the day Janet, to our great relief, remained stable . . . physically any way, although just what her mental condition was as I laid siege to her with an army of words and viewed every prolonged blink of her bleary eyes with suspicion, could only be wondered at.

During the night, I crept in and out of Jan's room to check her breathing with the result that she and Walt greeted the new day in far better condition than I did. The entry in my diary reads simply 'Jan fell in the dip' — I didn't need to write more for I'll never forget it.

The daily round of events at Aotea left little spare time but when I could, I'd climb the hills and watch the wildlife, especially the goats, which had been claiming more and more of my attention. Virtually undisturbed, they browsed in the scrub and rough pastures, their 'gobble-gobble' mating calls rising across the bay, their social groups so well defined, I could identify individuals from a distance.

Goats are fascinating creatures: gregarious, capricious, playful and intelligent. Beards flowing, the old gentlemen of the herd would join in the fun, rising on back legs, heads tilted to one side. Balancing like awkward ballerinas, they would crash to the ground, horns locked in mock combat.

Only when the does were in season did I observe any real conflict and this was limited to the breeding bucks fighting off the young and eager who challenged their dominance. Then the monarchs raced about, chasing any upstart with lowered heads and flashing eyes, daring the challenger to come near the doe whose tail swished seductively and whose bleating told of her desire, the unyielding call of the wild animal to propogate.

When the frenzy of mating was over and the kids were due five months later, I'd witness the birth of the wild goats. Little does heaving and straining, sometimes accompanied by screams of pain, then the minute creatures struggling to free themselves from the embryonic sacs. Within minutes they were on their feet, poking and butting the underside of Mama until they found the full and waiting teat. The little ones tested their legs with sideways leaps into nowhere and, as if a giant hiccup had seized them, would take to the air in an astonishing display of agility.

The wild sheep were more difficult to observe, their home being in an inaccessible part of the island, but I was permitted a few glimpses of the black beauties, whose lambs seemed fragile beyond description. I watched one day as a ewe dug a hole for her lamb with her front hoof. I could only guess at the reason. Perhaps it was to prevent the lamb rolling down the steep hill or was it for warmth, keeping the lamb below the level of the surface and away from the chilling winds?

The infants of both species were 'planted' by their mothers; some under fern or in the midst of stinging nettle. The baby goats often lay in little caves or in the shelter of a fallen tree. Some unspoken command and understanding compelled these infants to remain in their hiding places while the mothers went off to graze; many lay concealed for hours neither moving or calling out until they heard the familiar voice of their mothers.

Occasionally I'd meet with the wild pigs, usually lazing in the sun on the track. Although Grunt and Snort had never inspired fear, I was not so sure the behaviour of a wild pig would be as predictable and, from the various tales we'd heard of their ferocity, I felt no great desire to study them at close range. However, on one walk with my three terriers, I entered a clearing and before me stood a most magnificent sow and three piglets, the rays of sun through the trees illuminating the gold in their black and tan colouring. We were a mere three metres apart, but she made no move to run and I knew I hadn't a hope of outdistancing her even if I could have willed my feet to move. I moved nothing but my eyes, looking for a tree or even a stick should I have to defend myself. No suitable tree appeared in my line of vision nor could I see any weapon of defence. We just stood and looked at each other and, although I was very frightened, at the same time I could not help but admire her power and beauty.

'Hello,' came my husky voice. 'I won't hurt your babies.' I wished she could say something reassuring in response. Instead she shook her huge head menacingly and started pawing the ground. Now I was trembling and could almost feel those great jaws latching on to my thigh. I nearly fainted as she charged and I closed my eyes for the attack. I opened them as she sped past me, so close she brushed the hem of my jacket.

Mike, my Silky terrier, let out a terrified yelp as he was lifted from the ground by one deft scoop of her nose and sent hurtling down the embankment. Satisfied, the sow hurled herself around and, passing me at the same close proximity, gathered her offspring together and trotted off into the scrub! I almost cried with relief. She could so easily have savaged or even killed me, but she did not. Still trembling, but elated at the experience, I called the little dogs after me and headed for the safety of home.

On my return, I found Dan Freeman and a friend sitting in the lounge. Dan was an old friend from Te Anau and, before leaving New Zealand for an overseas trip, he had stopped in to visit and to bring his two sheepdogs to us for safekeeping.

While Dan and Val were with us, they helped change the exterior of the little grey house to an attractive colonial green, trimmed with white. The extra willing hands also helped us dig away some of the slip covering the back of the house — until then it had served as a ladder to the roof to deal with Bertha's ailing chimney.

Again the lowly wheelbarrow was brought into use and load after load was dumped over the embankment. Slowly we uncovered the back of the house, revealing a very sturdy and useful set of washtubs which had apparently been buried in the slip. These were installed in the laundry-storage room and Walt ran the necessary pipes to them with the intention of bringing the hot and cold water to the laundry once he had finished redecorating the bathroom.

This face-lifting had involved removing the bathtub which was situated at such a height from the floor it required pole-vaulting capabilities to enter and exit without breaking your neck. Besides that danger, there was never enough hot water to accommodate us all at the end of a day and we had decided a shower would replace the comfort of a leisurely soak. It was Mitch's idea and we happily consigned the job to him with very appreciable results. Next the room was painted and repaired and it was as Walt hammered the last few nails into the moulding that he hit the pipes carrying the water to basin, shower and, we hoped, the washtubs. By the time we tore off the moulding, removed the wallboard and found the puncture, the house was in flood.

Just as we were about to taste the sweet victory of a do-it-yourself bathroom, Walt had, with one finishing blow, turned it into a Keystone Cops movie complete with spurting water, mops and buckets as he played Peter and the Dyke with one hand and frantically waved orders with the other. Water flowed from the bathroom, into the kitchen and over the little step into the lounge faster than we could mop it up. The boys tried to remove the wallboard, working around Walt who was valiantly attempting to stem the flow. In the resulting turmoil, the three of them were squashed into the corner behind the toilet. The tangle of arms, wallboard, moulding, hammers, rags and spurting water in the confined area between the wall and toilet, reduced me to tears of laughter. Reaching over, around and under each other, the men managed to remove the wallboard, find the leak and stop it. The freshly-painted walls of the bathroom were now spotted and streaked and the curtains dripped into the four centimetres of water covering the floor. Various items floated about the pool that used to be our kitchen floor, gently tumbling over the little step into the lounge where they continued to bob about searching for dry land. All of us were, to a degree, rather wet, with Walt drenched from head to toe, as he took the full force of the 'Old Faithful' he had created. Now we had to re-do what we had just re-done. 'Not to worry, Mom!' said Mary as she waded past with a bucket and mop.

Walt had had better luck when he replaced most of the front wall of the lounge with sliding glass doors. The only danger we had been in was that the roof might cave in before he had built a suitable frame to accommodate the expanse of glass that would fill the room with sunlight and give us a dazzling view of the bay. For a considerable time, neither sunshine nor view was possible, thanks to the decorative abilities of Grunt and Snort who painted the outside of the doors with swirls of mud, reaching as far as their stretched bodies and indignant noses would take them. This left us with a view that resembled the inside of a mud pie and it wasn't until Grunt and Snort were evicted to greener pastures that we could fully appreciate this addition to Aotea.

We were quite pleased with our efforts thus far, even though some had to be repeated several times before completion. With the help of friends and the inventiveness of the children many changes had emerged, but our labour force was about to receive a blow, for Roy announced he was going fishing with a neighbour, which would mean long stretches away from home, and Mary had made the decision to leave for nursing training.

It came as a bit of a shock to learn that Aotea was not the beginning and end for all of us, and it was equally difficult for the children to express their dissatisfaction knowing how desperately we wanted them to stay. Here they were protected and sheltered from what I perceived to be damaging influences. We used all the time-honoured arguments parents through the ages have relied upon to persuade our impatient fledglings that they were too young to fly and face the world alone but, in the age-old tradition of the young, they longed to test their wings.

Mitch left too, but his venture was a cruise through the Pacific where he got his first taste of sailing. He returned four months later full of enthusiasm for wind power and with estimates of how much fuel we could save when, not if, we built our own yacht and sailed, free of charge, back and forth to Picton.

Walt dug his toes in on that one. He had tackled many construction tasks without knowing precisely what he was doing but building a yacht was beyond his ingenuity. It took a lot of persuasion to overcome Walt's reluctance, but aged opposition capitulated to youthful exuberance and the yacht, which was eventually christened *Aotea*, was begun.

None of the sheds was large enough to accommodate the boat and a platform had to be erected on the front lawn, one of the few flat areas available. This meant the work could progress only as the weather permitted but, in due course, the first boards were crossed and screwed together setting into motion an endeavour that was to test skills, resolve and tempers for many months to come.

Twenty-two months after her inception, the *Aotea* was lowered gently into the sea, but not before the hair-raising task of getting her from an upside-down position on the building platform to right-side-up on the beach had been completed. Running along beside her as she lumbered to the edge of the lawn supported by rollers, I was reminded of the Lilliputians trotting beside a sleeping Gulliver. As she nosed over the incline there was momentary alarm as one of the ropes restraining an over-enthusiastic descent gave an ominous 'twang'. Triceratops growled and Gulliver yawned, threatening to break our fragile hold as everyone rushed about shouting directions, the less confident declaring *Aotea* would be matchsticks or kindling before she ever tasted the sea. Moans of defeat gave way to shouts of victory as the remaining ropes held until she was safely nestled in the waiting cradle some ten metres below.

At high tide on Roy's 21st birthday, she was nudged from her cradle into the sea. Climbing aboard, amidst smiling congratulations from the 35 or so friends who had joined us for her christening, we took her on her maiden voyage around the bay, a beaming Mitch at the tiller.

Aotea now needed only two items to compliment her whole — sails and an auxillary motor. The sails were eventually purchased with the proceeds from the sale of our organically-grown garlic and, on one terrifyingly memorable night, Mitch headed home with the motor. This was to be last journey for our original boat, the *Sirius*, for it was felt she consumed too much fuel and, on completion of the yacht, she was to be sold.

It was about 8 in the evening when Mitch edged through the winter darkness of Queen Charlotte Sound, heading for home. Suddenly the night around him was shattered by a resounding explosion and *Sirius* was engulfed in flames. Stunned and singed, but otherwise unhurt, Mitch plunged into the frigid waters, struggling to swim from the burning boat. He managed to kick off his gumboots but was unable to free himself of his heavy over-garment. Its weight, plus the choppy seas, made swimming almost impossible. Getting his bearings, he moved slowly in what he hoped was the direction of land and prayed the ferry wasn't due, for he would be directly in its path.

Bill Peters thought at first that the bright light he could see was a boat's running light. Closer scrutiny revealed neither starboard nor port lights, but a boat ablaze. The baches of the Sounds were not usually occupied at that time of the year; Mitch owed his rescue to the fact that Bill and Trish, along with two of their sons, had decided to come to the Sounds at that particular time.

Racing for his little boat, Bill and his sons made for the burning *Sirius*, unaware that Mitch was in their path. Relief and concern shared equal billing when Mitch heard the approaching boat for he realised he would not be seen in the dark. He, treading water, and Bill's small boat took turns at disappearing into the canyons of water. The cold had sapped Mitch's strength but desperation forced his unwilling arms and legs to move. The will to survive brought reserves of strength which Mitch called upon, controlling any panic that could spell disaster. As Bill came slowly towards him, he managed to manoeuvre into a position of safety and, as Bill passed, Mitch called out and was heard. Strong arms hauled him aboard, the voices comforting and reassuring. Mitch had been in the sea for 30 minutes and was desperately cold, teeth chattering from both the exposure and the frightening experience. Safe in the warm confines of the Peters' cottage, Mitch was ushered into a steaming shower, where he remained for a long time, thawing frozen limbs and regaining circulation.

Walt and I waited at home, unaware of the drama that had taken place and listened with disbelief when Mitch rang and told us what had happened. Bill and Trish returned Mitch to us the next day and the first thing I noticed when he stepped ashore at Aotea was the colour of his eyes: they had turned a steely grey. I searched for words to express our gratitude to Bill, Trish and their sons but could do very little else but cry when I saw Mitch, and the full realisation that he could have died dawned on me. Trish hugged me with a mother's understanding of the emotion I was experiencing while Walt stood, his arm around Mitch's shoulder, speaking quietly with Bill and his own two sons.

It took Mitch many months to work through the experience and his eyes remained that strange, haunted grey for a very long time. Ever the pragmatist, he worried, once the initial shock was over, about the loss of the new motor which had sunk with the *Sirius* and was not insured, and fretted over the lost revenue from the intended sale of the old boat.

Friends rose to the occasion and helped us search for the wreckage with hopes of locating the sunken motor. A depth sounder was used to scour the coastline where the *Sirius* had last been seen burning. Several pieces of charred, scorched planking were found but nothing of the motor which had cost us $1400. With the *Sirius* gone, our motor added to Davy Jones' underwater treasure store and the *Aotea* not yet ready for full-time service, we were without transportation. A kind friend offered us his boat for the duration of our confinement but it was an offer we accepted with great reservations. The boat was small and would have to stay anchored on the mooring where *Sirius* had spent her last days. The yacht took up one side of the jetty and the other side had to remain clear for the mailboat and visitors.

Our misgivings were fulfilled when Old Man Southerly saw his chance for a bit of fun and settled in for a three-day blast. I was on my way to the shed to check the goats the morning after the storm hit and, looking out towards the mooring, stopped in my tracks, heartsick but not surprised to see the little boat upside down. With only a dinghy at our disposal, we had to wait out the full fury of the storm before we could row out to assess the damage. The boat itself could be salvaged, but on board had been a radio, uninsured, and valued at $700.

There were times when life at Aotea seemed too much and the 'enough is enough' feeling would take over and we'd long for the quiet life of town, traffic, gangs and ordinary everyday problems. But somehow we muddled through, never quite desperate enough to throw away all the years of hard work which, despite the setbacks, were beginning to show results.

Several new fences dotted the hillsides and our little ragtag band of sheep were thriving and reproducing. The terraced garden flourished and the house and outbuildings looked greenly colonial. A big cartwheel with kerosene lanterns hung from the ceiling, dominating the lounge and casting fanciful shadows on the warm wooden walls. Walt had built a large bookcase that filled one wall and it bulged with the classics, do-it-yourself books and books on natural healing methods.

A fireplace made the room cosy and welcoming. The bathroom was back in order and my washtubs now had hot and cold running water. Visitors slept in bunks made from trees, lulled to sleep by the gurglings of Mitch's wine maturing under the bed. Bertha, if not yet tamed, had at least become cooperative and the *Aotea* stood proudly bobbing by the jetty.

As far as the eye could see there was beauty, even when the storms roared about us. Walking through the hills, we could watch the wildlife and, on gentle days, lie amongst the grasses, feel the soft wind ripple over us and listen to the voices of the sea, trees and the birds.

The children seemed happy and came home often. Our needs were few as each of us grew in separate ways to a new maturity. We often received requests to write about our unconventional life and farming methods as if we were experts in the field, when in truth we were searching ourselves and it was very much a matter of trial and error.

One of our innovations was the use of garlic as a drench for the animals. This caused no end of head-shaking at the local pub and even more amazement when a television crew came to film us chopping up pounds and pounds of garlic, mixing it with paraffin and soap, then squirting it down the throats of our sheep! Another concoction that caused much head-shaking and, I suspect some head-holding, was Walt's home brew. 'The life-blood of Aotea', as it became known, is as wicked as a wayward genie in a bottle. It has been known to cure constipation, insomnia and cranky babies. It was also loved by Jody, my Arapawa goat, who would go to great lengths to sneak a sip or two or, if you weren't watchful, devour the entire contents, her muzzle deep inside the glass. Samantha preferred gin.

Walt's brew reached heights of renown when we had a visit from the Duke. Although used to champagne for breakfast and white wine with dinner, he was unprepared for the subtleties of taste and quality of aroma that bubbled forth from the yellow vat in the kitchen.

It was holiday time and it was decided we should have 'elevenses' so, on the dot of eleven, we brought forth our humble brew, which was all we had to offer and the Duke accepted a glass along with the others.

It so happened that Billy Jo, a new Arapawa kid, had joined my growing menagerie and had connected most painfully with an angry bee the day before, leaving her face swollen and distorted. True to my natural healing beliefs, I had made poultices of hot mashed potatoes, yoghurt and honey, which had proved an almost impossible concoction to apply. Therefore, I had wrapped her head in swaths of bandages from which the mixture dripped and oozed.

As the Duke launched into his third brew, which was lethal after two, Billy Jo, until now having lain unnoticed in a box in the corner, stood up, stretched and shook her head, spattering bits of mashed potato mixed with honeyed yoghurt for a considerable distance, her bandages slipping over one eye as she did so, giving her a ghoulish appearance.

Having consumed a goodly portion of his third brew, the Duke was no doubt seeing more than one apparition as Billy Jo rose and shook herself and the Duke looked aghast. He became even more wide-eyed when some of the goo was deposited in his lap as a result of the shaking. Hastening to reassure those present that the 'goo' was a mere collection of harmless ingredients and *not* the loathsome residue of an infection, which their faces clearly indicated they suspected, I unwound Billy's head, sponged away the remaining poultice and found the swelling gone and her beautiful face quite normal again.

By this time some of the guests had a distinctly greenish tinge and others moved uncomfortably in their chairs, looking down at their laps, lips tightly drawn and wearing the same incredulous look as had the electricians on seeing Walt sporting a trouser leg of cabbage leaves. I wiped down my bespattered guests, forgetting for the moment about Billy Jo, who should have been ushered to the great outdoors. To my embarrassment, she ambled into the centre of the room and proceeded to relieve herself, leaving a large, steaming pool, followed by the dropping of little pellets, staccato-fashion near and around the feet of my guests. I ran for the dustpan and scooped up the droppings. Then, with the sponge-mop, I tried to hide any trace of Billy's show of bad manners.

Some of our guests now rose and, stepping around the dark spot on the floor, took their leave. Not so the Duke! I think he was rather enchanted with watching what the simple folk do to wile away the hours.

Seemingly oblivious to the effects of the brew and the rising crescendo of an impending storm, our undaunted guests — the Duke and his party — lingered on until finally it was deemed wise to make a move before the weather deteriorated further.

'I say, old chap, do you think I could take a bottle of that exquisite refreshment with me?' asked our distinguished guest.

'Certainly,' replied Walt and went to the fridge for the departing gift.

The dinghy tied to the end of the jetty swung back and forth irritably as the wind licked its heels. The tide had fallen, providing a two-metre drop between jetty and dinghy. Just how we were going to deposit our merry friends into the boat from such a height was not altogether clear, for there seemed little likelihood of getting someone completely sober into the moving target swinging madly to and fro below, let alone a slightly tipsy blue blood.

We need not have concerned ourselves, for the Duke took matters into his own hands. Clutching the brew and waving a cheery farewell, he stepped off the jetty into space!

So suddenly did he depart that we had no time to assist or to bring the dinghy in closer. But, to our complete astonishment, he rose from the bottom of the boat where he had miraculously landed and with a beaming grin, thrust the bottle up at Walt. 'I say, old boy, would you open this for me?'

'Now?' asked Walt, still stunned by the Duke's dexterity.

'Most definitely now!' boomed the Duke.

Walt cracked the top with his knife and handed it to His Lordship who took a large gulp, whipped the outboard motor into action and disappeared in zig-zag fashion across the bay.

Not all of our visitors to Aotea were as memorable. In fact some of them — concerned with the wildlife — were becoming downright boorish. The interest in the wild sheep had sparked off a steady stream of scientists, individually and collectively, all showing great concern for the wild sheep, but also 'discovering' other aspects of Arapawa that had apparently gone unnoticed until now. There was a lot of vehement discussion about the bush and it was indicated that nothing other than the birdlife, snails and kiore (native rats) should legally be permitted to inhabit this area. That posed a dilemma as the wild sheep most certainly resided in part of it and had been declared 'special'.

Another point of interest was the presence of the goats and pigs and I became aware of a completely different inflection in the voices of the scientists when they spoke of these animals, for they were referred to as 'noxious, vermin and pests', while the bush and all else were spoken of in tones of reverence.

My mild objections were greeted with lectures on how I, a foreigner, could not possibly hope to understand the fragile New Zealand ecology and I received the distinct impression that my opinions were neither needed nor wanted. However, I continued to give them, especially when a report was made declaring the goats and pigs must be controlled and that it was planned to shoot the goats from a helicopter, then poison their carcasses with 1080 poison to kill the pigs!

To say I was horrified was putting it mildly, for having wished only to draw attention to the wild sheep, I had inadvertently brought a death sentence on the other wildlife I had come to love. I was warned in grave tones that, unless something was done, and done immediately, Arapawa Island was in danger of collapsing into Cook Strait, due to the depradations of the goats and pigs.

Timidly, I reminded the scientists that Arapawa had been grazed for a very long time by all sorts of animals roaming over the axial ridge in the absence of fences and invading and occupying the reserve. These included wild and domestic cattle, plus many thousands of sheep. Up until a few months ago no-one had known or cared about the bush, now suddenly goats and pigs had become public enemies and some people were getting hysterical about their presence on the island. How, I argued, could they say the condition of the bush had altered when they had just examined it for the first time; what was the standard of comparison?

Surely, I persisted, the animals and their surroundings must have come to some ecological balance in the two or more centuries they had co-existed? Why, if the numbers of wild animals were as they claimed so high, had the populations not spread over the entire island instead of remaining in a given area?

These and other queries were not happily received and again I was told that I should leave such decisions and judgments to those who were knowledgable in these matters. Obviously, they would have preferred it if I had retired into domestic oblivion and taken my questions and protests with me.

My own research into the history of the animals was never considered worth reading and even now has yet to be taken seriously, no doubt because much of it is in conflict with that of the scientists . . . the knowledgables . . . the men from the Ministry.

Initially, I pleaded for compassion, for leniency, for research into the possible scientific and historical significance of the goats and pigs as well as the sheep. I had nightmares about helicopters and 1080 poison. Then I happened to see a report that was marked 'Confidential'. Whether by chance or design, this document came before me, destroying what little was left of any rapport between myself and those who advocated 'control'.

At first, my opposition was not so much against the whole idea of control; I was more concerned with the methods and motivation. However, when I saw the confidential report, my stand for the animals changed and hardened. Until now, I had been kept informed of events and had received copies of reports and papers which I appreciated and acknowledged. Now, it seemed, because I had questioned the decisions, I was no longer to be involved. Things would continue to happen, only I would not know about them and, consequently, could not cause trouble. The confidential paper recommended, not control, but extermination. I felt I had been deliberately misled.

Writing to one of the men concerned, I demanded to know the truth of the matter and, because he had signed the paper, he had no choice but to admit extermination was what they wanted. Now I was past being horrified; I was angry, shattered and frightened for the animals. I tried to plead their case before the local body concerned with management of the portion of the island where many of the wild animals resided and was told: 'We don't want foreigners in here telling us what to do.'

Turning to the Forest Service, the 'agents' who would carry out the killings, I received more advice: 'You won't make a very good New Zealand citizen if you disagree with our policies'.

Writing and answering letters became a full-time occupation for me; letters to various Ministers and those that served under them, letters to the newspapers and letters to the Prime Minister, who seemed a bit confused as to which portfolio goats should be referred. I wrote to anyone vaguely connected with or interested in animals, in the hope of getting some help in my fight to save the Arapawa wildlife. What had begun so well with the wild sheep, now became a fully-fledged battle with the Marlborough Sounds Maritime Park Board and almost every government department. Usually at each other's throats, they banded together in collective security, bringing the full weight of bureaucracy against one lone woman and a herd of goats.

Alice in Wonderland had nothing on Betty in Bumbleland and there have been many times when I knew just how Alice must have felt. For while I wasn't surrounded by smiles from the Cheshire Cat or a cranky Queen of Hearts, there have been plenty of Tweeldedees and Tweedledums, with a few Mad Hatters thrown in for good measure.

I jumped into the big, dark hole of bureaucracy, chasing not the elusive rabbit, but in the hope of simple reason. It was not to be found.

CHAPTER VI

The Men From The Ministry

Having done business and battle with the Knowledgables of bureaucracy over the years, I have come to the conclusion that there are three main types. With a bit of practice, you can tell which one you are dealing with act accordingly.

If your encounter is a brief one, you probably won't get past the first type, but if it is of a protracted nature, you may well meet them all, several times around, starting with the foot soldiers and running through the ranks of the little generals, perhaps to Caesar himself.

The first I identified were the Lesser Knowledgables. 'Lesser' applies to mental capabilities as well as rank. They often twist uncomfortably in their chairs when confronted with questioning citizenry and, if holding a pencil, will most likely break it in two. A variation on the 'calm assurance' theme lies in folding a piece of paper until it is reduced to confetti, which they shower all over themselves. Sometimes this shredding is done under the desk, so look for tell-tale signs of paper around the chair. They usually are clad in field boots, shorts and bush shirt. Most seem to suffer from insecurity. Beer is their preferred drink.

Second are the Intellectual Knowledgables. They usually come equipped with an array of letters after their names, meant to inspire awe and place their opinions above question. They often smell of formaldehyde and seldom speak English, which precludes any possibility of being understood, and saves them the embarrassment of answering questions. They spend a great deal of time trying to outdo other Intellectual Knowledgables with their ability to identify every New Zealand tree and bird in Latin. There is great agitation if 'Aloada Rubbishii' is spotted and identified (in Latin, of course) before other Knowledgables see it. This is followed by copious note-taking. They drink white wine.

The third group comprises the Greater Knowledgables. They use copious quantities of men's deodorant and after-shave lotion and their attire ranges from rumpled suits to knee shorts, walking socks and neatly-pressed shirts. They are the 'super cools'.

Many Greater Knowls will sit on the edge of the desk, swinging a leg while talking. This gives them the advantage of height and adds to the super-cool image. If found sitting behind a desk, they will usually put their hands to their lips in prayer fashion and nod while listening to grievances, or sit back in the chair with thumb and index finger of each hand forming a circle, the index finger to lips. This preoccupation with the lips can be interpreted as the well-known 'lip service' most give to issues. Or perhaps they are keeping their fingers in their mouths in case they should say something that might get into print.

Greater Knowls are friendly folk and like to be called Big Brother to indicate their care and concern. They have a peculiar habit of carrying a big stick with a carrot dangling from the end. They drink gin or whisky.

All Knowledgables have one thing in common: a letter to the newspaper will throw them (and sometimes their whole department) into an advanced stage of apoplexy. Several letters to several papers can, I have observed, cause symptoms similar to pulpy kidney. Excessive amounts of leg paddling, bleating and champing of jaws must indeed sap their strength, which may account for their inability to think straight and make intelligent decisions.

I have come to the added conclusion that the energetic planting of pine trees is not, as they would have us believe, for export revenue, but to produce the reams of paper needed by the Knowledgables to write incoherent letters and jumbled reports.

In addition to my growing volume of correspondence, I was now invited to speak at various places around the country and gave at least one newspaper interview a week. Suddenly Arapawa had become synonymous with goats and any semblance of home life disappeared as I launched into a crusade that was to span ten years and is still unresolved. I was still naive enough in those days to believe that all that was needed to solve the conflict was to present the goats' case to someone who would understand and support me. There was one stipulation however: that someone had to be a Knowledgable, or at least a member of the inner circle of decision-makers.

What I found was that plenty of verbal support was given to me personally, but no-one was willing to present that support publicly. When I questioned them on this apparent lack of integrity, I invariably received the same pat answer: 'I have a wife and three children to support, Mrs Rowe.'

In other words, they either backed the official line or they were down the road, pink slip in hand. While I sympathised with their plight and took some heart from whispered conversations of support, I took great exception to the system that forced people into compromising situations and stifled freedom of expression with threats.

It was a crazy game we were playing; individuals cheering me on in private but condemning me publicly. How do you cope with a friendly enemy? Or was this part of the strategy to throw me off balance?

How did it change? One day I was merrily making my way through a life of self-sufficiency, happily oblivious to problems other than the immediate ones of survival, the next I was embroiled in a nasty running battle with bureaucracy. I exposed everything I could in letters to the papers hoping people would understand. It wasn't just the issue of the wildlife, but an issue of the way the system was run. If a herd of goats could cause government departments to become bellicose and heavy-handed, imagine what they'd do with more important issues.

One of my biggest problems was to try to get the opposition to look at the facts, rather than concentrating on me, the objector, for they seemed obsessed with my gender, my nationality and my mouth. Female I was, a New Zealander I had become and vocal I would continue to be. Changing from Yank to Kiwi did little to enhance my popularity or my right to ask questions. There appeared to be endless concentration on the individual and very little on the issue.

The clobbering machine moved into gear and I was directly in its path, along with the wildlife whose intended fate was a lot worse than mine. It was tempting at times to follow the oft-given advice of the opposition to sit down, keep quiet and let them do the thinking, especially when Big Brother started banging me over the head with the carrot and sometimes the stick as well, but then I'd look at the Arapawas and know they had no voice but mine.

One day I was sitting in the lounge with two Forest Service officers who had come to inform me that the shooting was to go ahead, when our conversation was interrupted by the arrival of the mailboat and a very interesting letter. It contained a copy of an article about work being carried out in England in an attempt to breed back to the Old English goat which had now become extinct in its native land. In the article was a description of the Old English which fitted the Arapawa goats perfectly.

My own research had shown that goats had been released on the island by Captain James Cook on several occasions and had been

Mitch.

Yvonne was among the first to heed the call of the Arapawas. She and Ashley have played a vital part in the battle to save the Arapawa wildlife. Here Yvonne carries a goat down the track leading to the jetty in front of the Aotea homestead. I follow close behind with another.

Once the poultry department became established, it reproduced with amazing rapidity until Aotea cheeped, chirped and gobbled with an assortment of chickens, ducks and turkeys, each vying for a place on the front doorstep. While eggs remained in short supply, the birds heeded the command to go forth and multiply.

observed by Edward Jerningham Wakefield in 1839. I soon realised that the Arapawa goats could well be the sole survivors of the Old English breed. Even though it was only a theory, it certainly seemed enough to halt any action against them until some research could be done.

I pointed this out to the Forest Service officers who sat, unimpressed and disinterested. 'Surely this will make a difference?' I pleaded, but their answer was 'No'.

It seemed they would happily exterminate what could be the last survivors of a breed. All at the expense of an unsuspecting public.

My theory was reinforced by a letter from a surprise source — one of the Knowledgables! They were not having much success researching the wild sheep, but did I know that 'James Cook released goats in an isolated corner of East Bay in June of 1777'? This was one for the books — our scientists pointing out the possible historic significance of the goats to themselves, then refusing to follow up their own leads. Yet with nothing known about the wild sheep, they were granted protection. For the sake of the sheep, I was pleased but I simply could not understand the absolute refusal to grant the goats the same grace. When I mentioned this discrepancy to the chairman of the Park Board, his reply was that it was a 'numbers' game'. If there were more sheep than goats, then the sheep would be shot!

I received a reply to a letter I wrote to the Rare Breeds Survival Trust in England, concerning the goats. It said: 'From the evidence available to me, the Arapawa Island goats probably represent an important surviving repository of the genes of this old breed. The conservation of such a breeding group is very much in line with the principles guiding the activities of this trust . . . I hope very much that the Arapawa goats can be saved'.

I forwarded a copy to the then Minister of Lands and Survey, Mr Venn Young, who replied: 'I regret that the letter you enclosed from the Rare Breeds Survival Trust Ltd is merely opinion and I suggest you contact the D.S.I.R. for advice on the significance of these animals'.

To leave no stone unturned, I wrote to the D.S.I.R. and received this answer: 'Beaglehole has Captain Cook recording in his log that goats were put ashore in Queen Charlotte Sound on what must have been Arapawa Island. Cook also records that the Maoris did not kill and eat goats of the second liberation. Whether the Maoris restrained themselves later we do not know. I have no later reports about goats being set ashore, but it is likely . . .'.

I went back to the Minister who then wrote that he wanted more time to 'deal objectively' with opposing points of view and the investigation would take longer than expected.

While he was dealing objectively, I wrote to the Prime Minister. His reply only added to the confusion: 'I will ask the Minister of Lands to consult with the Minister of Science and to let you have further comment. Your letter has been forwarded accordingly'.

That phrase 'forwarded accordingly' always worries me, for it translates as 'your letter is well and truly lost in the maze, never to be seen again'.

This round robin of letter writing went on and on with such a conflicting array of answers it was impossible to break the code. All the while, the time for the extermination of the goats and pigs was drawing near.

I wrote out a resumé of my theory and research, and sent it to the Department of Lands and Survey. This time I was not ignored, nor did I receive the usual 'Thank you for your interesting letter' put-off. This time I received a visitation.

Three men arrived looking most uncomfortable after a bumpy trip to East Bay. To help them regain their equilibrium I served lunch and a cup of tea. Then I launched into my defence, or rather the animals' defence. I pointed out to them the privilege we had of saving a species thought to be extinct; that perhaps we had discovered a living museum, a monument to the past. Not only did we have a privilege, we had a responsibility to see that these animals were not wiped out by bumbling bureaucracy.

Instead of sharing my joy of discovery, they declared the matter was no concern of theirs and it mattered not if the goats were of great antiquity, for the island would be much better off without them. They went on to say that the 'park land' of Arapawa needed to be cleared of animals. The 'park land' to which they were referring was the reserve which has a topography fit only for a mountain gorilla and could hardly be called a park! Once again, I heard the story that New Zealand had evolved without the presence of browsing animals and once again I was excused for not knowing this as I was a 'foreigner'.

The lecture ended with a reference to the law, the gist of it being that no introduced animals were permitted within a reserve and since the goats sometimes occupied the reserve, they were guilty until proven innocent.

'Gentlemen,' I chimed in sweetly, 'the wild sheep are introduced and have been allowed to remain in the reserve.'

That must be, I thought, a temporary oversight on their part. One couldn't expect them to remember everything. But Knowledgables do not like to be bothered with trivia. I thought the violent reaction that followed was due to my impertinence in jogging their memories, but no, it was due to the fact that I had drawn a parallel between the goats and the sheep. This analogy has always produced pulpy kidney symptoms in Knowledgables, much as it did that day. It seems to be a very sensitive point.

After the initial rush of blood they calmed down enough to assure me that the sheep were to remain because of their antiquity and long association with the island.

'How long have they been here?' I ventured.

'At least 130 years,' came the solemn pronouncement.

'It is possible the goats have been here over 200 years,' I said and they sat back, putting fingers to lips.

'Mrs Rowe,' droned one with infinite patience, 'it has been said that five Angora bucks were released on the island 50 years ago. So you see, my dear, the breed simply cannot be pure!' He smiled a charming smile and rose to leave as if there was no more to be said.

'But,' I persisted, 'the wild sheep have been associated with the domestic sheep of the island for, what did you say, 130 years, but that doesn't seem to prejudice their case for purity.'

Heaving a sigh and resuming their seats they tried another tack. The sheep were a rare breed and endangered species, hence of special interest.

At this point I pulled out the letter concerning the Arapawa goats' connection with the extinct Old English breed and, waving it under their noses, countered: 'Our island goats may well be the sole survivors of the Old English goat, now extinct. And as for endangered, I see nothing safe about looking down the barrel of a government shooter's rifle!'

It all seemed pretty basic to me, but the Knowledgables kept bringing up the law, departmental policies, ruined vegetation and, last but not least, the recent finding (they would not tell me by whom) that Arapawa Island was in imminent danger of falling into Cook Strait . . . all because of the goats.

'Gentlemen, as I perceive the problem, you have one policy for sheep and another for goats. Very old rare breeds of sheep are acceptable in the reserve, despite the law, while very old rare breeds of goats are not acceptable because of the law!'

I looked from one to the other, my gaze resting on the man who seemed to be the senior member. He lowered his eyes and busied himself by wiping the palms of his hands on the knees of his rumpled suit.

It has always surprised me to see just how quickly and easily brash self-confidence turns to nervous indigestion, or in this case, sweaty palms, simply because you ask questions. I deemed it my right to ask questions about such apparent absurdities, but they obviously did not; they were the Knowledgables.

Trying to get the conversation going again, I gushed 'I know that this is a dumb question,' — then hesitated as if too embarrassed to ask it — 'but, aren't you breaking your own law?'

A look of surprised hurt crossed their faces. 'We are not breaking the law, Mrs Rowe,' the senior one responded to the charge, 'merely bending it.'

'Well then, why not bend it for the goats?' It seemed simple enough.

'Mrs Rowe, bending the law for the sheep is one thing, but breaking it for the goats is quite another!' He said it with such conviction, I think he really believed he'd said something profound and beautiful.

'I see,' I said, while at the same time shaking my head negatively, the negative-positive reaction betraying my state of confusion. 'I see,' I repeated. Then, as if engaged in an argument with myself, blurted out, in rather unladylike tones, 'NO, I DON'T SEE!'

It seemed the Knowledgables had themselves a problem and it wasn't me. What they had was a policy so inflexible that any challenge to it could not be accommodated without fiddling, so fiddle they did, only they called it bending.

When I suggested what was good for the goose (in this case, sheep) was good for the gander (goats), and that we start at the very beginning, the men of the double-talk moved towards the door. Realising they had failed in their mission to convince me that black was white, they tried the 'might is right' pitch as a parting salvo.

'You know, Mrs Rowe, you won't make a very good New Zealand citizen.'

'I know,' I replied hotly. 'I've been told that several times before. And,' I added, 'you don't like foreigners coming in here and telling you what to do, do you?'

This brought nods of agreement all around.

I clenched my fist to control my rising temper and said, 'Gentlemen, before you ring the immigration office and have my passport revoked, let me assure you I am only trying to clarify the picture. Somehow all of this doesn't add up.'

One Knowledgable summed it all up for me with his parting remark: 'Madam, I think you are on an ego trip!' And, having satisfied themselves that I was suffering from delusions of grandeur and incapable of grasping even simple facts, they guided one another to the boat.

I fumed as I thought of the various encounters I'd had. I had held more intelligent conversations with my children when they were pre-schoolers, yet these people were running around loose making policies.

Not everyone loves a stirrer and some people who knew us suddenly didn't want to anymore. With each newspaper article or letter, our popularity rating dropped. It was particularly upsetting when the children came home from a trip to town with tales of being verbally abused on the streets because of my stand. I came home in tears on many occasions, provoked by the 'dear hearts and gentle people' who didn't like goats or foreigners.

For months I had been crossing Cook Strait on a regular basis, attending endless meetings, conferences and seminars, plus fulfilling speaking engagements, always with one cause — the plight of the animals.

The last trip had left me so exhausted, I promised myself and the family I'd declare a truce with the Knowledgables and take a much-needed break. The family had begun making not so discreet noises about my preoccupation with the wildlife and how much more I was needed at home.

That last trip was like many before — days filled with fruitless meetings and encounters with Ministers and Members of Parliament who suddenly remembered they had an art gallery to open whenever I walked into their offices. In one day alone, I repeated the Arapawa story 15 times and began to feel like a programmed robot, only I wasn't able to press a button and start the tape over . . . 'In 1777 Captain Cook released goats . . .' No, I had to think. answer questions, stand up to television scrutiny and do my best to sound fresh and convincing.

As I trudged up the long incline to the home of a friend where I was to spend the night, I felt as if I'd been on the witness stand for days, and I looked forward to an evening's rest.

Terry made me a hot herbal tea, massaged my back to ease the tension, put me to bed with a gentle touch and soothing words, then closed the door softly behind her. I sank back into the pillows, savouring the quiet, the tea and the delicious anticipation of sleep after the disappointments of the day.

Drifting deeper and deeper into that area of free floating before the final curtain falls, I hung suspended, totally relaxed. Suddenly the door slammed against the wall with such force that I sat bolt upright in bed — just in time to see Luke, the puppy, followed by Martin, Terry's eight-year-old son, disappear beneath the bed, both yelping uproariously.

Leaning over to see what was happening below, I was met head-on, or rather nose-on, by the antenna on Martin's walkie-talkie which painfully penetrated my nostril.

'007 . . . 007, do you hear me?' Martin roared into the walkie-talkie, as he emerged from under the bed in pursuit of the barking puppy. Escaping his tormentor, Luke bounded across the bed. Martin followed and in three gigantic leaps, using the bed as a trampoline, once again landed on the floor, diving under the footboard to repeat the whole performance.

'007 . . . 007,' demanded Martin, while Luke barked incessantly, and the walkie-talkie crackled with static.

Meanwhile, I was still dangling head down, bottom up, over the bed with a bloody nose. I hauled myself back on to the bed to be met by the second wave of Luke and Martin and was swept along with the tide to the floor.

Surely, I thought, Terry and Craig must have heard the commotion and I wondered why they hadn't been in to see what had befallen their house guest. I plugged my nose with a piece of tissue and stumbled down the passage towards the kitchen where I found Terry blissfully feeding carrots and celery into the juicer which was drowning out all other sounds.

Quietly closing the kitchen door, I searched for Craig in the hope someone would take this erring child from under my bed and I could get some sleep. The sound of music came floating along the passage and I paused before the ornate doors that led to the lounge. The floor shook as the volume and intensity of sound increased behind the closed doors. Timidly I knocked and, unheard, knocked again. This time the doors were flung open and I was nearly swept off my feet by the power and thunder of a Wagnerian opera playing at full volume. Craig pulled me into the room to share his ecstacy and whirled about conducting the orchestra, using a wooden spoon for a baton.

As if in response to the command for crescendo, Martin and Luke poured through the french doors, just missing a whack across the ear from Craig's downbeat with the wooden spoon. I stood dabbing my nose with a piece of tissue as around me swirled Luke, Martin, Craig and a whole host of 'heavies' from Wagner.

I spoke Craig's name as he stood in the centre of the room, flapping his arms like a giant condor, but no sound could be heard and, since he had closed his eyes in rapture at the music, he couldn't even read my lips. I headed wearily for my room determined that I would deal with Martin myself, should he come looking for James Bond in my bedroom again. I stopped at the bathroom to wash the blood from my face and, as I leaned over the basin, heard an ominous 'click'. Trying the door, I found it securely locked.

'007 . . . 007, where are you?' Then the answering snap, crackle and pop of the walkie-talkie on the other side of the door.

'That wretched child has locked me in,' I thought and pounded furiously on the door. Craig probably thought it was the bass drums responding to his latest directive with the wooden spoon, and as far as I knew, Terry was still feeding her hungry juicer oblivious to all else. I'd just have to wait until one of them came to the bathroom.

'Betty, Betty, are you in there?' I certainly was, but just how long I'd been there was not clear, for as I lifted my head to respond to the pounding on the door, I realised I had fallen asleep on the bathroom floor while waiting to be rescued.

'Yes, I'm here, but I'm locked in. I can't get out!' I said somewhat dramatically, hoping to be there when Craig's baton met Martin's bottom.

'You've locked it from the inside,' said Terry. 'It's a self-locking door, so you won't be disturbed when bathing!'

Poor Martin, I hadn't even given him the benefit of the doubt and without so much as a struggle, I had accepted my fate and presumed Martin was guilty. Feeling a bit foolish, I fumbled with the lock and opened the door.

Terry looked at me with a puzzled expression. 'Betty, is everything all right? I went to the bedroom and found the sheets and blankets on the floor . . . and there was blood . . .'

I opened my mouth to explain, but instead just shook my head and pointed to my nose.

In the morning, Terry and I rehearsed our lines for the visit to the Knowledgables. I fortified myself with two tumblers of celery and carrot juice, and mentally prepared arguments for a more reasonable and humane approach to the Arapawa wildlife.

I had become increasingly concerned about a bureaucracy that kept cloning itself and churning out think-alikes. Individuality seemed a dispensable commodity; rhetoric, prejudice and uncompromising officialdom prevailed.

If thoughts on the subjects of research, ethics or conversation crossed the bureaucratic mind, they were quickly submerged. It seemed that minds involved in the larger philosophies of party politics or winning the next election found little time for the trivia of reason. So it had gone on, meeting after meeting, but this one was not without humour. Six of us sat wrangling over the fate of the goats; Terry and I for the animals, four officials from various departments, against. One of the Knowledgables had evidently decided some fresh approach was needed and turned to me with: 'The problem, Mrs Rowe, is that the goats are eating all the grass.'

For the past few years, I had been told the problem was they weren't eating enough grass, but preferred the bush. Now, according to the experts, they had suddenly changed their dietary habits and invaded the grasslands. Obviously, the goats were not meant to eat at all, for it seemed eating grass was almost as bad as eating bush. I had my mouth open and my finger poised, ready to reply when the Knowledgable on my right leaned over to address me. He had not heard the remarks of his colleague, or I assumed he had not, for this would have made his contribution all the more inane. 'Of course, if the goats were eating grass and not bush, there would be no problem,' he informed me, smiling.

I looked from one to the other, my mouth still hanging open, speechless.

Knowledgable No. 1 looked as if he'd like to punch No. 2 and hunched in his chair with a considerable amount of egg on his face. This mind-boggling intellectual exchange had my head spinning and I wondered how many hard-earned taxpayers' dollars had gone into the pay packets of these two men.

I took no pity on the squirming Knowledgables and reminded them of the advice they had so often given me — gems such as 'You'd better get your act together, Mrs Rowe.' Addressing the disgruntled official on my left, I asked: 'Now, just what is it, bush or grass?'

'Grass,' he snapped, jamming his hands in his pockets and slumping further in his chair.

'Bush?' I asked with a nod to my right and received an enthusiastic endorsement.

Well, I thought, if I can't get them to agree with each other, how can I ever expect them to agree with me, and I trudged wearily from yet another encounter with the Men from the Ministry.

Terry took me to the ferry and, finding myself a quiet corner, I curled into a ball and slept the entire three-and-a-half hours to Picton. Another three hours brought me home to the shores of Aotea from which I determined I would not roam, at least, not for a while. I unpacked and put my suitcase in the wardrobe, slamming the door with a resounding bang as a symbolic gesture of finality. Exchanging knowledge with the Knowledgables had left me with an urgent need and a deep conviction; the need was for peace and quiet, an escape from their inane burblings; the conviction was for the preservation of the Arapawa wildlife, despite the ineptitude and ignorance I had encountered.

Unfortunately, peace there could not be, for the powers-that-be felt threatened and, peering out from their turrets, perceived the enemy and it was me, backed up by sheep, goats and pigs. The 'machine' was swung into action to crush resistance once and for all.

There were rumours of public censure, phone calls, more visitations and the threat of being investigated by the S.I.S! I was told I would be most unwise to ignore the messages from on high, although just what the penalty for insubordination was to be was not clear.

The Minister in charge of this whole affair seemed incapable or unwilling to 'deal objectively' and it was small wonder, for even the opinions of his trusted officers were varied and confused.

'The goats must go, but the sheep are valuable.' (D.S.I.R.)

'Here, here,' cried another. 'Far too valuable and intensely interesting.'

'Well,' timidly offered a botanist, 'sheep eat trees too, therefore the wild sheep pose a threat to the vegetation. I think they should go.'

'The sheep must not be disturbed!' commanded a Lands and Survey Knowledgable.

'I don't think we should worry about the sheep,' came the helpful remark from the Forest Service, for by now they had joined in the melee to assure the Minister they would happily shoot the sheep as well as the other wildlife on the island.

'We only want control.' (Park Board).

'I prefer not to change the word "exterminate" in my motion to the board.' That also from the Park Board who seemed incapable of understanding the consequences of their actions during the entire saga.

'The goats are only scrubbers. Nothing more!' declared the Forest Service, without looking at a shred of evidence to the contrary.

'We must preserve these rare and unique goats for their genetic and historic qualities.' I suspect the Knowledgable from the Lands Department who made that statement was handed his pink slip and sent to McMurdo Sound on a PEP scheme for committing the heresy of defending the goats.

The last two proclamations came from departments sporting the same Minister! Tally-ho, taxpayers' money alive and well in the Think Tank. How could the Minister go wrong with such clear and concise opinions from his merry men?

Just how the Minister resolved the conflict within his information service was most interesting. The taxpayers were to foot the bill for one department to shoot the goats, while another department was to be rescuing them in the next gully with a helicopter; also at the taxpayers' expense!

The Knowledgables weren't agreeing with me, but they weren't taking any chances . . . just in case I was right after all. The order went out to capture 100 Arapawa goats.

If the goats were 'just scrubbers', why was public money to be spent to save them? If they were not 'just scrubbers', why was public money to be spent to kill them?

If, as the Forest Service claimed, they could get better goats at the freezing works, why did they spend thousands of dollars to capture and breed the Arapawa goats to 'preserve the gene pool'? How do you preserve the gene pool of old scrubbers; more importantly, why?

Balderdash and ballyhoo. But all was not lost. Suddenly, I wasn't alone anymore; the Beautiful People had begun to come forward, people who cared, people of compassion. They may have been few in number, but to me they were like the legions of Rome.

CHAPTER VII

The Beautiful People

Who needs them? Why save them? What good are they? Must the survival of an animal depend on its use to the human race or can we accept it for itself and allow it a place to live in peace? I have always maintained that the Arapawa wildlife have the right to life not only because they are rare and unique, but because they are living, breathing creatures.

Many people began to heed the call of the Arapawas. It was a gentle dawning of awareness. Some rallied because it was something special, others were in pursuit of justice for the animals simply because they were oppressed. Each of the Beautiful People who came to Arapawa Island could perhaps tell you what is was that prompted him or her to join such an improbable cause. I can but tell you what they accomplished . . . and it was grand.

'Keep them coming! Don't let them stop or they'll break back!' So came the cries from the tops of Arapawa's remote hills.

I strained my eyes for a sign of movement along the horizon as I waited below, concealed in a cluster of bushes. 'Dear God,' I begged, 'please let us catch them,' hoping that the prayer of a wayward agnostic would reach the right place. I had pleaded with the Keeper of forest and glen for a solution many times before, and now there were a magnificent 11 people struggling through high fern and prickly gorse in an attempt to save the wild goats of Arapawa. For a fleeting moment, the silhouettes of men, women and dogs were visible where the sky meets the mountain tops, then they disappeared into the valleys, the sounds of the chase echoing off the ridges into silence, and I was left to watch and wait.

I sank back against the bushes and closed my eyes, listening carefully for even the faintest sound to indicate what was happening. Only the weening of the gulls and the sign of the wind-ruffled grass could be heard and in time my thoughts wandered back to the events that had brought us to this moment of adventure.

Mike Willis, Director of the Willowbank Wildlife Reserve, Christchurch, had answered my letter of desperation and had been one of the few people who took my fight for the wildlife seriously. Most of the replies I received to my appeals for help had been politely negative, or in some cases, outright rebuffs. Had I been championing whales, dolphins, kangaroos or the giant panda, I would have been received with open arms, but a plea on behalf of a herd of introduced goats was unthinkable and, I gathered, unheard of.

Whatever I wrote to Mike must have served to rouse his curiosity, for in due course he arrived at Aotea and stood on the jetty with all the makings and markings of Mitch's twin brother. I smothered him with hours of verbal and written information, trying to condense many years of research about the Arapawa wildlife into something concise and coherent. However, I fear I succeeded only in overwhelming him with tales of numbskulled Knowledgables, bumbling Government departments and Captain Cook's wise intentions.

Sitting in the lounge, home brew in hand, bathed in the gentle light of the kerosene lanterns suspended from the cartwheel, we talked, or rather I talked and Mike listened, into the small hours of the morning. Mike did not try to dissuade me from my crusade; instead he joined it and became a major force behind the attempts to save the wildlife. He left for home with wild sheep and goats for his reserve and a commitment to their survival.

Was it fate, destiny, luck, predestination? Call it what you will, but when the photographs of the animals Mike had taken to his reserve appeared in the Christchurch papers, they coincided with information received from England by a New Zealand goat breeder concerning the efforts being made to breed back to the extinct Old English goat. It was the same information as I had received.

This goat enthusiast took the time to travel to the reserve and see the Arapawa goats for herself. Her response was electric — the Arapawas were a perfect match with the description of the hitherto 'extinct' Old English. My theory was confirmed by someone who knew more about goats than all the Knowledgables put together. However, it made not the slightest impression; on the contrary, it seemed to intensify the efforts being made to exterminate them!

The persistent jangle of the telephone had woken me from a sound sleep. In those days, phone conversations were impossible after 5.30 p.m. when the island's generators were turned on, somehow interfering with the cables. On lifting the receiver, we often heard the sounds of far-off electric drills or power saws, but rarely voices.

On this particular night, it was only through the efforts of the obliging operator who relayed every word spoken from the caller to me and back again that I was able to determine a Mrs Calcutt wanted 200 Arapawa goats. She had heard the goats were to be slaughtered and, since she and her husband were having difficulties in obtaining stock for a goat-farming venture, thought they might be able to capture some Arapawas. It would save a reasonable number of the animals from slaughter.

Tolls relayed not only my words, but my complete surprise when the figure 200 was mentioned.

'Two hundred?' I shouted.

'Did you really want 200?' shouted Tolls obligingly.

The three of us agreed this was the figure and, with much ado, I managed to give Mike Willis' name and phone number, with instructions to ring him and see what could be done. Perhaps some of the goats would be saved, but just how we would get them from Arapawa to Akaroa I would have to leave in Mike's capable hands.

Mike had risen to the challenge posed by Mrs Calcutt's request and placed an advertisement in the newspaper for recruits to muster goats on Arapawa Island. The response was not fantastic but a handful had come forward. Now this little band of men and women were racing about the hills of Arapawa with absolutely no knowledge of the terrain and no experience in mustering goats, but they were giving their all.

I was startled from my daydreaming by the strident voices of men and the urgent barking of the dogs as once again they came into view. This time they were hard on the heels of a group of goats that were spiralling their way down the hill, the bucks stopping to lock horns, betraying their uneasiness and fright. I had remained below and hidden in order to position Samantha and Jody as decoys with the hope that once the wild goats got near enough they would see them and head their way rather than bolt back over the ridge. It took much prodding, pushing, cajoling and swearing to get my decoys into a position where they would be seen. Quickly tethering them to a bit of scrub, I dived into the bushes out of sight.

Samantha obligingly bellowed in indignation which served to attract the descending herd. They hesitated for a moment then, with the volunteers hard on their heels, blocking escape, headed for Sam and Jody.

Samantha sensed the excitement in the air and strained at the rope that held her. Jody looked up to see a swirl of caprine aunts, uncles and cousins by the dozens heading straight for her and she, too, struggled in alarm. Crawling on my stomach, commando style, I reached the two pets and released them, then jumped to my feet and raced in the direction of Aotea, calling to Sam and Jody as I ran; down the hill, across the paddock, over the little bridge that Mitch had built, into 'Homebreak Paddock', only daring to look over my shoulder to see if the goats were following. They were.

I gulped in some air, tasting the musty scent of goat and willed my legs to a faster pace. Sam and Jody were terrified and doubled their efforts to get to home and safety. No doubt my performance heightened their anxiety and the three of us soon had the wild goats rushing pell-mell to catch us. I felt like the Pied Piper with a stampeding herd of beautiful wild animals strung out behind me. Only I wasn't playing a flute, just wheezing and gasping in rhythm with my pounding heart and feet. Together we ran into the waiting yards and tears sprang to my eyes as I hugged Sam and Jody who stood quivering by my side. They were tears of exultation, joy and momentary victory.

For those who had laboured on the hill, it was a great moment. We handed out the brew for the hot, dusty volunteers who sat smiling and satisfied, watching the goats inspect the confines of the yard which was to be their home for an entire week.

Our jubilation soon faded when the first of the bucks sailed quite effortlessly over the fence in a bid for freedom, followed by several more in quick succession. The chase was on again and we began the task of rounding up escapees and endeavouring to erect makeshift barricades.

Very soon, a problem of even greater proportions presented itself. We hadn't realised that the time chosen for the muster coincided with kidding and on the first night, many of the babies began entering the world, several prematurely, as a result of the stress put upon the mothers.

Hastily we made up individual pens from bales of hay for the mothers and new-born, turning the top shed into a caprine maternity home. A tarpaulin was stretched across the yards to provide shelter for the remaining goats and the volunteers brought hay, leaves, branches and willow bark for the goats to eat and finally managed to settle them down for the night. Our gestures of goodwill seemed to reduce their fright and some sat chewing their cuds, watching us, no doubt pondering the folly of man and, I guessed, longing for the familiar safety of their mountain home. Sadly, I thought, they would never again know the freedom of truly wild creatures, for man had decreed that henceforth they would suffer either capture or death.

Yvonne and Ashley were two of the volunteers who had come from Christchurch and from this chance encounter has grown a lasting and warm friendship, spanning many years and many battles for the Arapawa wildlife. It was Yvonne's training as a nurse that proved invaluable as she, Ashley and I spent most nights sitting by Little Bertha with the premature babies in an effort to save them. Other volunteers took turns sleeping in the shed with the maternity group, keeping mothers and babies together, feeding and watering one and all. The gentleness of the volunteers was a touching and beautiful thing that restored my faith in human compassion. The fact that the majority of the goats survived was due to the care these people gave so willingly day and night.

On the sixth day the punt arrived to take the goats to the mainland. It was a bitter-sweet day for us all; sweet in the knowledge that some of the goats would be going to a safe home with the Calcutts, bitter that we had to go to such extremes and put the goats through so much to save them. Seeing them huddled in the corner of the yards, pawns in the power play of Big Brother, made anger well up within me.

Mike and I selected a fine buck (we christened him Arapawa Bill) and several does in order to preserve the breed, for there was no guarantee that those going to the Calcutts would remain pure.

While the goats were gently urged into the woolshed in preparation for loading on to the punt, I wandered to the top shed that had been the scene of such a beautiful outpouring of love and compassion for the beleagured goats. Sitting amongst the bales of hay, the musky scent of goat everywhere, I felt the week catch up with me. I was tired, so very tired; bones and muscles aching and sore, but the mental fatigue was greater.

Gale, who had also come from Christchurch, came and sat next to me, holding my hands in hers. Words weren't necessary; we had shared in a special event. Shared also was the sadness that the goats still had a long way to go before it was over. If only we could explain to them that we were trying to help.

As the voices of the men rose from the woolshed, we knew the time had come to load the punt. It was inevitable that the goats would be frightened. Every effort was made to ease their plight and, one by one, they were put into pens aboard the punt. It was all over. We had done what we could.

Our parting with the volunteers was tearful and emotional. A week ago we had been strangers, now we were old friends, a bond forged through mutual caring. Aotea seemed strangely quiet when everyone had gone. Walt and the boys began tidying up the sheds and I walked up into the yards which, moments before, had been alive with activity. Strange, I could still see the goats watching me, shadows in the corners of the yards; questioning eyes, frightened, even at our attempts at kindness; little new-borns teetering on spindly legs as their nervous mothers urged them away from us. Bucks, proud and majestic, leaping fences in defiance. Haunted, I sank into a bale of hay and, sobbing, fell asleep.

The men left me there, knowing I wanted to be alone. Hours later, Walt came and sat beside me, trying to understand my grief, yet unable to comprehend. He, Mitch and Roy had laboured alongside the volunteers all week, neglecting the farm and garden. Our 'quiet life' had been violently disrupted by my preoccupation with the wildlife and hundreds of hard-earned dollars had been paid out for huge phone and postage bills as I sought help for the animals.

I learned later that the volunteers had done even more. Ashley and Yvonne had struggled for hours to keep the babies alive and warm. Driving home in torrential rain, they fought fatigue and frustration, stopping at times to try to coax the primus into life in order to warm the honey and water we had mixed for the infants. Despite their efforts, some of the kids had died, leaving these two loving and compassionate people desolate. They crawled into bed at 4.30 the next morning.

Ken, a trooper all the way, rode in the truck with the goats as they made their way on the long, slow trip south. They stopped in Christchurch to unload the goats meant for Willowbank Wildlife Reserve and ate a meal prepared by Kathy Willis at 3.30 a.m. From Willowbank, the remainder of the animals, accompanied by Ken, lumbered on to Akaroa. There was a return trip to Christchurch for Ken before he could collapse into bed.

It was a brave saga, seen to its conclusion by the first of the Beautiful People who heard the call of the Arapawas and answered. Some months later, Ashley, now a fully-fledged member of the Arapawa rescue team, and I journeyed to Wellington to confront the high lamas in their temples.

The first thing we did was to get lost and, at the appointed time, found ourselves many kilometres from our destination. This delayed the meeting by several hours until we were rescued and ushered into the holy of holies.

There was tension in the room as we set about presenting our case.

The predominently black and ten coloration of the wild pigs is demonstrated in this photo, with the less frequently coloured ginger type in evidence. Some research in Britain has potentially identified these animals as resembling the Old English Forest Pig, but to date very little is known about the Arapawa wild pig.

There is more than one way to carry and goat and John Simister of Staglands and Rick Denton find back packing these newly captured goats an easier way of bringing them to Aotea.

A noble Arapawa Island ram from the herd at Aotea. This fellow has been recently shorn precluding the usual shoddy appearance of the wild sheep that annually shed their fleece. Poaching and indifference in official circles conspire to make the future of these animals uncertain.

Infrequent visitors to Aotea — wild pigs in the back yard.

It was obvious from the start that our host would have been quite happy had Ashley and I managed to remain lost permanently!

In his agitation, Greater Knowl chewed the end off his pencil before he broke it in two. Reinforcements were called and we were joined by a bespectacled and bearded Intellectual Knowl.

Now, two Knowls make a mountain of resistance, and before long the conversation had degenerated into a shouting match.

'I think you'd better leave!' panted the High Lama as he stood to dismiss us.

Ashley's brown eyes fairly danced as he ignored the dismissal and proceeded to remind our host that he was a public servant and we paid his salary! This statement, I have observed during various encounters, never fails to provoke a response, usually registered at a high voice level, and this was no exception.

Having completely lost his super-cool image, the Greater Knowl shouted at Ashley across the desk and I went to the window to regain my composure, arms tightly crossed, biting my lip and tapping my toe.

'Now, Mrs Rowe, don't get in a huff.' It sounded like a command.

Turning from the window, I smiled sweetly: 'I'm not in a huff at all,' I said in a sugary voice, then exploded: 'but I am furious!'

A considerable free-for-all followed with voices reaching new heights as the argument raged. During the loudest exchanges our host cast anxious glances in the direction of the outer office as if expecting reinforcements.

Exasperated, I rushed to the desk, threw my papers in the briefcase, steamed past Ashley who was still undefeated, and flung open the door. I had to step back to avoid the avalanche of bodies that fell into the room in a jumble of arms and legs, hands still cupped to their ears!

Greater Knowl turned purple with rage, his eyes popping and his neck swelling above the collar of his neatly pressed shirt as he vented his spleen on his staff as they picked themselves up from the floor. Stepping over these soon-to-be-redundant bodies, we stormed down the hall. Someone trotted after us pleading that we stay for a cup of tea which we haughtily declined.

'Can we take you to the station?' I wondered why all this sudden concern for our welfare. Perhaps they didn't want to be left alone with Greater Knowl. Whatever the reason, I just wanted to get out of there as fast as I could and, turning on our heels with a 'No, thank you, we'll walk!' we stomped off.

It didn't take us long to discover that the station was many kilometres away and my high stepping exit, so full of pride and passion, soon turned to an agonising limp as blisters formed in my neat little 'town shoes'. Back in the centre of the city and somewhat recovered, we decided we needed a drink and headed for the 1860 bar, ordered three vodkas and proceeded to drown our sorrows.

It was late when we emerged on to the deserted Wellington streets and arm in arm, blisters and all, we skipped to the railway station where we somehow managed to catch the right train for Ngaio. Between hiccups and giggles, we recalled those poor people we left staring up into the purple face of the Greater Knowl and wondered if they would be hung, drawn and quartered or simply whipped before joining the dole queue.

'May I have your ticket?' came a voice at our side.

Ashley looked up with a sheepish grin and shrugged his shoulders. 'What tickie?'

Glancing from Ashley to me with a disapproving scowl and putting his hands on his hips, the conductor boomed: 'Your train tickie, that's what tickie!'

His strident tones turned the heads of our fellow passengers who watched as we fumbled and giggled, searching pockets and bags for the elusive 'tickie', which we finally produced. Steadying each other, we lurched down the aisle, with the unsmiling looks of the more temperate following our progress.

The walk to Bet's house sobered us enough to recite the events of the day and, despite the hour, Bet decided we must compose a letter of indignation then and there.

Ashley paced around the table like a greyhound on course, trying to collect his thoughts and put them into some semblance of indignation. I had slumped into a chair, eyelids at half-mast, feeling weary and battle-scarred. I wondered if democracy gave this to everyone: the freedom to knock your head against a brick wall.

Ashley cleared his throat and began: 'Dear Sir,' which Bet hurriedly typed, anticipating his words of wrath.

It was not to be, for we were burned out from the privilege of exercising our freedom of speech. After one lap around the table, Ashley made a left turn instead of a right one and, stretching full length on the couch, fell fast asleep. Bet looked at me expectantly, but, kissing her fondly on the cheek, I too deserted her, overcome with fatigue.

I received a letter some time later from a friend with his finger on the pulse and an ear for the unusual happenings around town.

He wrote in large exaggerated letters, punctuated with three exclamation marks: 'I HEAR YOUR VISIT MADE QUITE AN IMPRESSION!!!' And I've no doubt it did.

CHAPTER VII

Strange Happenings

The collective effort of numerous people resulted in a moratorium being granted to the wildlife, allowing more time for research on our part and a chance for the government to distance itself from the bad publicity it had been receiving over its handling of the Arapawa problem.

Sitting once again with various officials, I had been surprised to hear that we would have six months' grace. No sooner were the words out of the chairman's mouth, than the Conservator changed it to a year. My gratitude for this magnanimous gesture was soon dimmed when I realised that the expiry date for the moratorium coincided with the introduction of the Wild Animals Control Bill, which would, in effect, allow them to do anything they saw fit. I should have guessed there would be a method in their madness.

However, a temporary relapse into insanity on the part of the Knowledgables did have some welcome side effects, apart from giving the animals a year's lease on life; it allowed me a much-needed breathing space after the constant lobbying and travelling to Never-Never land, sparing me the necessity of arranging my life around ferry schedules and speaking engagements. I felt like I'd been away a very long time and it was good to be back into a routine, if you could call the erratic happenings at Aotea 'routine'.

Nothing proved such a diversion from my preoccupation with the wildlife as the growing awareness that we were sharing Aotea not only with an assortment of two- and four-legged creatures, but also with a host of unseen, though often heard, cohabitants.

My first encounter came in the quiet of an early summer morning. The sun had yet to make an appearance, but the breeze through the open window was already hot and humid. We had risen before dawn so that the men could get away for an early sheep muster and avoid the heat of the day.

Enjoying my solitude, I decided to play Eve in my morning Garden of Eden and stripped down to the barest essentials. To add to the feeling of total freedom and my bohemian mood, I even removed the partial dental plate that fills in the gap where nature has denied me the growth of two second teeth. With gaping grin and clad only in undies, I was happily pottering away in the kitchen when to my horror I heard voices approaching on the path leading to the house. They sounded very near indeed and I panicked at my semi-nakedness and the welcoming smile that would be minus two prominent ivories.

To get to the clothing and the teeth, I had to pass through the lounge, where the ranch-slider doors would put me on full display. Chances of a quick cover-up diminished as the voices drew rapidly closer, so I darted into the bathroom and wrapped a towel around me, sarong style, wondering where on earth these people had come from. No boat had arrived and the dwelling in the next bay was seldom used. There was little chance of anyone arriving in the adjoining bay without being detected unless they came in the dead of night.

It was now possible to distinguish two, possibly three, women's voices, chattering and laughing as if sharing a happy moment, and from the clarity of their voices, I guessed they must be on the doorstep. I peered around the archway between the kitchen and lounge, fully expecting to see them. But there was no sign of them, so I sprinted to the bedroom and made myself socially acceptable.

The voices could not have been more distinct had we been engaged in direct conversation, yet the elusive callers refused to allow me the benefit of pinpointing their whereabouts. Whoever and wherever they were, one thing was certain; they had excellent voice projection, for to be heard so clearly yet remain unseen was quite remarkable.

Never mind, the mystery would soon be solved and I would know who came bearing such happy tidings in the early morning light. My welcoming smile, now with a full compliment of pearlies, faded when, as I stepped through the door exuding welcoming charm, the voices stopped and I was left smiling at the ngaio tree.

Running first to the back of the house to see if my friends had gone walkabout, I then raced to the head of the bay almost desperate to find visible bodies to attach to the voices, but I could neither see nor hear any sign of my visitors.

Perhaps, I thought, walking slowly back to the house, I had been invaded by talking myna birds! No, I assured myself, the radio had not been on. I struggled to rationalise what I knew I'd heard with what I hadn't seen. There must be a reasonable explanation.

Then I realised that the terriers, who always set up a fearful din when people arrived, had remained silent during the whole episode. Obviously, they had not heard anything to rouse them from their peaceful dreams on the couch. Several times that day, I rang the bach in the next bay hoping to solve the mystery, but the phone went unanswered.

Hearing bodiless voices on a single occasion was one thing, but when it happened again it became a bit unnerving. Again the voices approached in the early morning when I was alone. Needless to say, I wasted no time in rushing to catch my visitors before they could get away, only to find that as I stepped amidst their laughter, the sounds ceased just as abruptly as on the previous occasion.

My reports on the encounters, or should I say non-encounters, have met with varying responses. Some people tut-tut and mumble something about the strain of fighting with Knowledgables; others show interest and nod their heads to indicate they have had similar experiences. Since then the voices have come on many occasions and are not confined to early morning visitations nor to myself alone, for others, aware of the mystery and aura of Arapawa, have been allowed a glimpse into the unknown. For some it is frightening but I do not find it so. When I spoke to a Maori friend about it, she listened patiently and said it was 'Just the Old People'. She assured me there was nothing to fear.

The voices are not confined to the homestead path, either, for, as I walked in the woods one day, I heard the sounds of children at play. The happy squeals of the childlike voices came from my left and I turned from the usual path and moved deeper into the bush towards them. Although I walked for what seemed an eternity, I could get no closer to the sounds that lured me on.

When I stopped to assess the situation, I had an overwhelming feeling I was hopelessly lost. The trees seemed unlike any I'd seen before and there was no familiar landmark. As I stood there wondering if I'd stepped into another dimension, the voices of the children came towards me until the air around me was filled with the bell-like laughter and happy chatterings of youngsters at play. After my previous experiences, I knew they would probably not materialise. So I simply stood there and listened, until with an abruptness I'd come to expect, the sounds ceased.

Moments later I stepped out on to a ridge high above the homestead, although I'd been unaware of climbing to any height. What amazed me was that I could have reached such a lofty position with apparent ease for the trip down was both hazardous and difficult.

Shortly after my daughter-in-law came to live on the island, she and Mary were caught up in an experience that attested to the presence of men amongst our unseen guests. Marcia was in the lounge and Mary in the shower at Aotea when both overheard male voices engaged in conversation. Since there is a window in the bathroom that would allow Mary to speak to someone without leaving the confines of the shower, Marcia presumed she was doing just that, while Mary could hear the male voices clearly above the noise of the running water.

Both girls assumed one of the men in the family was speaking with the other and it was not until later when Marcia casually asked Mary to whom she had been speaking so long while in the shower, and had received a blank, puzzled look, that any further thought was given to the owners of these male voices. Mary assured Marcia she had not spoken to anyone through the bathroom window and Marcia assured Mary she had remained alone in the lounge.

The men of the family were rounded up for questioning as to their whereabouts during the hours in question. All were able to verify their absence and none of them had passed or paused for so much as a 'hello', much less a prolonged conversation as overheard by Mary and Marcia.

We were left with only one explanation — the unseen women and children of Aotea had not left their menfolk behind.

Not all the visitations occurred during the day; some were in the night. Perhaps the oddest happening was that concerning a UBO (Unidentified Bobbing Object).

Walt and I were on the deck of a friend's yacht saying goodnight after a lovely dinner and evening together, when Alan looked towards Aotea and saw the light.

'Hello, hello, what's that?' he asked, pointing to a greenish-blue globe that bobbed gently up and down in front of the house and, as we watched, moved slowly in the direction of the greenhouse. The first assumption was that someone had arrived while we were below deck having dinner, but it seemed strange we had not heard a motor since the mooring was not far from the homestead. Perhaps a boat had broken down and the occupants had been forced to row (which would explain their arriving unobserved) and with the light of a very weak torch were looking for help.

'Hello! Who's there?' we hollered through cupped hands to the globe as it passed in front of the greenhouse. There was no reply.

'It must be a sheep,' ventured Shalene.

'With one greeny-blue eye?' I countered with raised eyebrows.

There was an uneasy silence as we stood and watched, then Alan gave a relieved chuckle. 'It's just the reflection of the mast light in the windows of the greenhouse!'

This explanation was accepted happily until we realised the 'reflection' was continuing in places where no glass was present.

Our UBO could not be dismissed either as Venus, Mars or Jupiter on the horizon, a one-eyed sheep, reflections where they couldn't reflect and even the weak torch theory didn't hold much water.

There appeared to be only one way to find out and that was to head for Aotea and confront the mystery. With only a kerosene lantern to guide us, we edged through the starless night, trying to keep in sight the globe which by now had reached the bottom of the front lawn.

Although the air was still and windless, a sudden gust of wind, like someone's breath on a candle, extinguished our lantern light and we lost our sense of direction. The night was so black that even the familiar outlines of the hills were obscured and we had only the light from the yacht to use as a reference point.

While I fumbled with the lantern on the floor of the dinghy, Walt rowed slowly and cautiously, muttering at my inability to relight the lantern. I had no sooner succeeded and settled on to the seat when I was returned to the floor, joined by Walt, and we were plunged into darkness again. We had, with navigational expertise, beached ourselves on the rocks and the jolt had sent us sprawling in a jumble of oars, rope, arms and legs. To add to the confusion, the lantern had slipped from my hand.

Fumbling about in the dark, we located the lantern and, after much bumping into each other, filling our boots with water and tripping over the slippery rocks, we managed to get ourselves launched and drifted about aimlessly until we nearly decapitated ourselves as we rowed under the jetty. At least now we knew where we were and with all the confusion and noise we had managed to create, our unwelcome guest would know too.

Just before beaching ourselves on the rocks, we had seen the globe moving slowly over the gate and heading for the top shed. Then we had lost sight of it and our antics in the bay had precluded any chance of 'sneaking up' for a confrontation.

Once we were safely on the beach, I managed to relight the lantern and, with a good deal of apprehension, we headed for the top shed. I held the lamp high, leaving Walt with two arms free for battle should the need arise and we wondered whether or not to be thankful that all the children were away. Their absence would ensure their safety but, if things got out of hand, two brawny young men would be more help to Walt than I would, especially as I was already too frightened to speak.

Samantha and Jody were now sleeping in the shed along with several other orphaned Arapawa goats, but no sound of animals, disturbed or otherwise, could be heard, only an eerie silence. We moved slowly through the gate and into the yards and, as the circle of light reached the little clearing outside the shed, there stood Sam and Jody, trembling and shaking with such force as to be visible in the dim glow of the lantern. I managed a husky whisper and they came to me, obviously frightened. The actions of the goats made us all the more uneasy and it all seemed slightly crazy; creeping around with our little lantern, looking for someone with an equally dim light. If we did find someone, it was going to be a shadowy confrontation.

We stepped gingerly into the shed to find the other animals had fled into the night. The lantern cast shadows on the old beams and rafters, turning stacks of wood and discarded farm materials into sinister and threatening shapes. Our over-stimulated imaginations gave life to these inanimate objects and I picked up a pitchfork to do battle with a menacing sack of barley meal.

The top shed is divided in half by a waist-high wall — the only place left the culprit to be lurking if indeed he was in the shed at all! Armed with pitchfork and a stout axe handle, we advanced. When Walt gave the signal, I swung the lantern into the darkness created by the dividing wall. Walt stood poised to 'dong' any intruder as I played the light over the contents of the shed.

We stood with tensed muscles, barely breathing, when a noise from the other end of the shed caused us to whip around in alarm. Walt narrowly missed being punctured by my pitchfork in the process and I gasped to see a pair of beady eyes staring at me from the rafters above. I'm certain my heart skipped several beats in the few seconds it took to determine the eyes belonged to a disturbed rat that had scuttled away at our intrusion.

Stumbling down to the woolshed, like Holmes and Watson, we found nothing more menacing than our own fired imaginations and turned our attention to the house.

Due to some mechanical problem, the generator had to be cranked by hand and since I hadn't the strength to do this, we decided, after whispered consultation, that Walt would have to do the cranking and I would proceed to the house and flick on the lights.

The thought of entering the house was as spine-chilling as our advance on the shed had been, only this time I would be alone while Walt's crankings and chuggings and thumpings were enough to alert a whole army of burglars.

With a very good impersonation of the Cowardly Lion of Oz, I made my way to the house, slid open the doors and stepped inside. The anticipation of finding someone there almost paralysed me. When the 'genny' had reached what sounded like the proper crescendo, I flipped the switch and waited for Walt to appear. Together we searched under beds, in wardrobes, behind furniture and doors until we were satisfied no-one was present.

Walt thought we should go outside and look around once more but some cowardly intuition made me yearn for rooms where light filled all the corners, and we eventually went to bed with all lights blazing except in the bedroom where we slept but fitfully, jumping up and arming ourselves at every noise throughout the night. Our friends from the yacht arrived early next morning to see if we were all right. They had, from their vantage point on the water, been able to observe the globe move past the top shed and out along the track and then disappear. Walt and I had assumed 'It' had entered the shed and we had crept around in a cold sweat for nothing, playing cops and robbers and working ourselves into a paranoid state.

The origin of 'It' was never discovered for the light has never returned to Aotea unless it do so when unobserved. Whether it was animal, vegetable, mineral or of the spirit offered tantalizing speculation and, while the experience shook us at the time, it left no lasting fear, only curiosity.

Rex, a frequent visitor to Aotea, was a bit sceptical about all these stories of bobbing lights and mysterious voices until he had his own unusual experience.

Returning from a walk, he came into the woolshed where Mitch and Walt were shearing. The usually calm, cool and collected Rex was in a state of high excitement for, while he had long ago learned, like the rest of us, that the unexpected is often the norm at Aotea, he had not been prepared for the events that had sent him scurrying home from his morning walk.

'You'll never guess what I've just seen!'

The accent was on the 'never' and Rex took a physical step backward in disbelief when Mitch, without missing a stroke, answered calmly: 'The disappearing island.'

'How did you know?' Now the accent was on every word.

Straightening up, Mitch exchanged puzzled looks with Rex. 'I don't really know why I said that. It just came into my mind.'

No stranger to Arapawa, Rex had followed a route to the tops that he had taken many times before. Reaching the summit, he was confronted by a strange and unfamiliar sight, and his first reaction was to assume he had somehow taken a wrong turn and emerged further north than he had thought.

On closer examination, he found he was indeed exactly where he had first assumed he was, but there in the water stood a body of land separated from Arapawa by a narrow neck of sea. The island was fairly large and bush-clad and Rex was aware of bird life among the trees.

Not one to be easily startled and frightened, Rex had surveyed his surroundings and studied the little island for some time before deciding to retrace his steps and return for another look. This he did, only to find the island was no longer where it had been ten minutes before.

Rex was able to produce a clear and concise drawing of the island and its relationship to Arapawa. Unfortunately, he did not have his camera with him to capture it on film, but I wondered if it would have shown up even if he had managed to photograph it. The disappearing island has been seen by several people who report similar stories of coming upon a land mass in a place where nothing before had been seen and the accompanying feeling that they were in a strange place.

In his book, *Ke Puta Te Wairau*, W.J. Elvy describes in vivid detail some of his own encounters with ghost ships and long-departed souls on Arapawa Island. Dr Elvy's strange and wonderful experiences on the island were my first introductions to the legend and history of Arapawa and further readings about the area have confirmed it as a place of special significance.

Pits, mounds, middens and artifacts attest to an occupation dating back many centuries, long before Captains Cook and Furneaux rowed into East Bay to release livestock. Arapawa, at its northern extremity, wraps its protective arm around East Bay forming an open-air amphitheatre, shielding it from the full force of the elements experienced in Cook Strait.

Looking back into the midsts of time we can see a longboat making its way with a cargo of animals intended for release. This time they would not be given directly to the natives, but released in a 'secluded corner of East Bay . . .'.

Of this venture, Captain Cook wrote: ' . . . so that we have reason to hope this country will, in time, be stocked with these animals, if they are not destroyed by the natives before they become wild. But as the natives know nothing of their being left behind, it may be some time before they are discovered'.

Pigs, goats and sheep were set free on the east side of the sound, which is Arapawa Island. I wonder how Captain Cook would have reacted to the dilemma his generous gifts had caused, gifts sent by King George III for the people of New Zealand and the South Seas. Despite the captain's belief that the animals would be in no danger, their future now hung in the balance. The threat came, not from the natives, but from a conglomeration of Knowledgables as one-eyed as our UBO and twice as baffling.

The moratorium was drawing to a close.

CHAPTER IX

For Posterity

The voices from the past were infinitely easier to reconcile than the rumblings emanating from Bumbleland. Now the authorities had decided that we had had enough time to compile our research and, since they had no intention of reading it anyway, they began sending letters of warning that the countdown had begun and High Noon was approaching.

By a series of unplanned manoeuvres we had managed to keep the Forest Service shooters away from the wildlife far longer than the propounders of the kill intended, using the borrowed time for collating our research and, with all the prospects of finding a needle in a haystack, hoping to discover someone in the corridors of power with enough guts and understanding to respond. From the local level to the Beehive, even the best brains seemed incapable of addressing the problem from any point other than the sights of a rifle, and no amount of persuasion, friendly or otherwise, could wrest this frontier attitude from the gun-slinging Knowledgables. While Tweedledee shuffled papers and Tweedledum planned the offensive against the wildlife, Mike and Kathy Willis were busy with more constructive activities.

It was into their capable hands that the organisation of the second rescue attempt fell. They arrived with 25 men and women and proceeded to turn Aotea into a tent city for the second time.

Among the arrivals were some of the familiar faces from the first muster. For a growing number of people, chasing wildlife around the hills of Arapawa was getting to be a habit and we were bolstered by the newcomers' confidence and determination, not to mention the greater flexibility afforded by the added numbers. More people would enable us to cover the area thoroughly without the goats eluding us.

Camp was made behind the 'old house', this time spreading further into the bush and the shelter of the ancient trees surrounding the deserted homestead on the adjoining property. 'His' and 'Hers' holes were dug, old doors from the house made into tables and the outdoor kitchen organised under the supervision of Bob McDonald, whose job it would be to feed this hungry horde at all times of the day and night. Crates of beer were placed in the creek for cooling and sheltered niches were found for the dogs. Some people, disdaining the comfort of the tents, arranged their beds under the stars.

Everyone was up and ready to go as the dawn brought the promise of a hot, sunny day and, with it the additional prospect of dehydration and discomfort to those of us familiar with the rough slog ahead. Yet it was with that particular exhilaration generated by a common cause and intensified by the urgency of our mission that we advanced upward. The ascent was devoid of conversation as every breath was needed for the climb and, having reached the tops, we separated into two groups, wished each other luck and trudged our way through the bush in search of wildlife.

A low estimate of several thousand goats had been issued by the Knowledgables without the benefit of a count or survey, but the munching hordes eluded even the most skilled and practised eyes of the bushmen among us, leaving us with the distinct impression that such numbers existed only in the minds and wishful thinking of the opposition.

The uncompromising sun and the rough terrain produced a weary group of blistered, perspiring, dehydrated volunteers and only a handful of goats which refused to be mustered and had to be caught individually or in small groups of two or three.

Someone came up with the idea that on the outer reaches of the island (in the northern entrance) would be the place to find the goats, as they would be relatively undisturbed except for the odd hunter or Sunday boatie who thought it 'sport' to take pot shots at goats on the cliffs from their runabouts.

The plan was discussed as we sat around the campfire, sharing aches and pains, ideas, cold beer and the first of Bob's culinary delights. The strategy born from such ingredients was to erect on the beach a catching pen which the goats would be encouraged to enter, whereupon they could be caught, trussed and transported to safety. It was a plan we should have discussed with the goats, for they would have saved us a lot of trouble by declaring their complete opposition to such folly.

John Leary, from Wellington, had kindly donated his yacht for the entire week, placing it and his crew at our disposal. Just how we would have managed all the comings and goings with only our little *Aotea* for transport, I cannot imagine. The *Moonraker* took aboard a cargo of men and fencing materials and made the slow passage to Oamaru Bay in the northern entrance where an elaborate catching pen was erected. Those not involved with this operation combed the hills for the elusive goats, again with little success.

The following morning was bright and clear where we were, but a thick haze and mist covered the tops of Arapawa and we could only hope the sun, which even at this early hour blazed through the ring of whipped-cream-covered hill tops, would burn the white crown away and allow us to find our quarry.

Visibility remained zero with the volunteers playing hide and seek with each other and the goats. It was the dogs, whose closer proximity to the ground allowed them to see where they were going, that eventually sniffed out a small herd of Arapawas and started them running. Mustering goats on a clear day has its drawbacks but trying to determine what is happening in the fog is almost impossible. The dogs managed to hold some of the goats against the fence line and, with instructions from their owners, brought them below the hanging clouds where they were eventually joined by volunteers who tumbled into the light at various points and formed a cordon.

Those of us on the beach had been able to hear the hollering from the tops as the musterers endeavoured to keep in touch with each other in the mist, but we had no idea where they were or exactly where the descent was taking place. We scrambled to position ourselves at the best possible vantage points and with us scrambled some journalists who had come for a story and action photographs. Action they got, perhaps more than they bargained for, but in the melee that followed the intrepid woman photographer captured the excitement and confusion with expertise.

Once the goats and their escorts were spotted, all attention was turned to guiding the goats to the waiting pen which they were assiduously avoiding. This conflict of interests could have only one outcome and before long several people were in the sea struggling with goats who felt drowning was better than capture. I sat dripping and heaving on the beach holding a sodden, terrified young buck whose struggles plastered both our wet bodies with sand which soon dried in the merciless sun, leaving us encrusted like veal cutlets ready for frying.

Around me raced men, women, dogs and goats, and human shouts mingled with the shrieks of the animals. But most of the goats raced back into the protecting mists and the catching pen stood empty.

All that remained was to get ourselves, the dogs and the trussed animals out to the *Moonraker* anchored some way off the beach. We launched the dinghy into the pounding surf which glued our clothing even more tightly to our salted, sand-coated bodies and Mike and I were rowed out to the yacht to receive the goats which were brought to us in pairs.

Mike gave each goat a sedative to calm it and we placed them under an awning, covering them with a canvas to keep their body temperatures as constant as possible, for there was danger of chilling or overheating while under the effect of the drug.

Some of the volunteers found the energy to swim out to the boat to help speed up our departure. Not all of the dogs thought that a very good idea and tried to climb on the backs of their owners. Stripped to their underwear, bleeding from the piggy-back attempts of the dogs and burping swallowed sea water, volunteers swarmed aboard the *Moonraker* like half-naked pirates. Finding all present and accounted for, John disappeared into the bowels of the yacht, returning seconds later looking grim and disgruntled; *Moonraker* refused to start.

This was one for the books. We sat in the blazing sun in various stages of discomfort from our encounters with sea and sand, nursing 20 thrashing goats who threatened to hurl themselves overboard as they struggled with the effects of the tranquiliser. Home was a three-hour trip away and *Moonraker* had picked this time to go on strike!

For 20 minutes we sat in the sweltering heat, covering and uncovering the goats, while the men held a conference, trying various means to coax the yacht into life. A sigh of relief rippled through the bedraggled assembly of housewives, lawyers, farmers, carpenters and students who made up this rescue team as *Moonraker* throbbed and shuddered, then settled into a reassuring chug. The anchor was hauled aboard and we slowly drifted past the hills of Arapawa heading for East Bay.

Though we had had enough adventure for one day, the journey home was far from restful. Aside from the constant care of hot and cold goats, some with a spread of horns that could prove lethal in their semi-drugged state, a doe lying at Kathy's feet showed clear signs of labour. We had been careful to choose a time that would not present the problems of the first muster, when the does had been so near to kidding, but the stresses of this muster had triggered an abortion in the doe and we could only watch helplessly as she passed the barely-formed foetus from her body, giving comfort to her as we could.

Once we were safely tied up at the jetty, the goats were carried to the yards where they recovered from the last effects of the drug,

The law demanded we ear-tag the goats before release and some of the gentle hearts among the volunteers broke as the goats screamed more in fright than in pain. Note tag on doe in centre of photo.

In this amazing photo we can see across Totoranui (or Queen Charlotte Sound) to West Bay, better known as Resolution Bay. Captain Cook careened his ships on numerous occasions at Ship Cove, just north of Resolution Bay and rowed across to the east side of the sounds which must have been Arapawa Island. In the foreground lies Aotea homestead, (centre right), the House of the 500-metre Revolt and behind the trees in centre foreground the old homestead on Otanerau.

Lindsay Smith rows three unwilling goats and me out to where the Moonraker awaits her cargo of goats, volunteers and dogs to be taken back to Aotea from Omaru Bay.

Walt scans the hillside for signs of wild sheep or goats while sheepdogs Bo and Crib wait for the command.

staggering to their feet and shaking their heads to clear befuddled brains. The doe was treated by Mike and recovered from her ordeal. The press, who had been with us the entire day, now sought an interview with Mike and me. While cameras flashed and pencils scribbled on paper, we recited for the hundredth time our belief in the need to preserve the Arapawa wildlife for posterity. A sympathetic and understanding press printed a two-page story, complete with action-filled photographs; a tribute to the enormous outflow of compassion and concern, which far outweighed the exhaustion and discomfort experienced on this mission of mercy.

The second muster had not brought in vast numbers of goats, indeed there were under 100, but in terms of comradeship and a meeting of minds, it excelled anything we had expected. There were moments of understanding between strangers born of a common endeavour; men with the gentleness of women, tending the frightened animals with a touching tenderness, and women standing up to the rigours of the muster and wearing blisters and scars of the hunt befitting any man of strength.

While our main occupation centred around caring for the captured goats, with daily forays to the tops to search for more, there was time for fun and fellowship. The aroma of coffee and sausages simmering on the fire as we sat under a canopy of twinkling stars at the end of a strenuous day brought out tales of the day's adventures. Some spoke with a reverence of the encounter with pigs, goats and sheep found grazing peacefully together in a clearing, presenting a picture from the Garden of Eden. The volunteers stood and watched this scene quite awed by the beauty and tranquility of undisturbed nature; the animals unaware of the storm building around them in Wellington. There were swims at night with the moon leaving paths of light across the bay and two of the men came streaking into the camp one night, causing a lot of good-natured screaming and racing after the culprits.

All of us remember the second muster with great warmth, a sharing of purpose and adventure; our parting free of the emotion that brought the first muster to a close. Several people offered their boats as transportation for the goats and another group of animals made their way to safety.

Some nine months later, wondering if we were destined to spend our 'getting-away-from-it' years fighting with Knowledgables and rescuing wildlife, we prepared for yet another muster. This would be, by far, our most ambitious attempt and the last chance before the shooters arrived.

It was a diverse group of 45 men and women that arrived at Aotea, each nurturing his or her individual ideas about what should be done and by what means. We had among us members of Greenpeace and other organisations with animal welfare uppermost in their minds. Others came to rescue as many animals as possible because of their rarity and were committed to conservation rather than animal rights. As the week developed, it seemed some had joined to make mischief and sow discord but, despite the varied personalities and motivations, the group managed to bring 114 goats on to Aotea in an effort that was the most physically exhausting of all the musters.

Prior to the arrival of the 45 musterers, a group of old Arapawa wildlife friends had come to Aotea to prepare the most elaborate plan we had tried thus far. We electrified our existing sheep fences by adding a homemade outrigger that ran through many kilometres of freshly-cleared scrub and connected with a small hydro built, with Kiwi ingenuity, from a bicycle dynamo. This created an area in which we hoped to contain the goats.

The next stage of the plan was to erect a catching pen on the ridge and I watched as Yvonne, with calm deliberation, carried a full roll of netting up the steep hillside, moving with the grace of a goddess, dressed in gumboots and an old dress, while I struggled with a mere half roll, cursing those who had made all this necessary. Once we had the equipment at the top, the men, with ropes around their waists, drove posts into the steep slopes of the cliffs overlooking Cook Strait and a netting fence was secured to the bottom of the posts and laid back flat on the ground.

The plan we had devised was to divide into three groups. The first team would begin to muster from the northern-most area in which the goats were to be found, driving them over the flattened fence and into the waiting arms of the second group in the southern part of the reserve. Once the goats had passed out of sight and sound, the third team would scramble down and erect the fence, camouflaging it with cut manuka branches. When the signal was given the goats would be turned back and once they came to the fence would, as goats do, head up and into the catching pen. Samantha and Jody were to be used as decoys again.

With the electric fencing completed and the catching pen in place, we had only to await the arrival of the volunteers and set into motion this elaborate rescue plan. Once again, a large boat was donated for the cause and it deposited the men and women on the beaches of

Aotea complete with enough equipment and food for a week. Until things were sorted out, it looked a bit like the Marines had landed and Tent City resembled a metropolis when compared with the first humble gathering of volunteers.

Celia and Sid, an English couple, had recently come to live with us and their presence allowed the family to be more involved with the rescue attempt, as Sid kept the home fires burning and Celia had meals prepared and looked after the house and animals.

With walkie-talkies to keep us in touch, we split into three groups, piled into *Aotea* and the other donated boat and sailed off for East Bay. Sam and Jody displayed their anxiety at the strange faces, unfamiliar dogs and sea travel by trying to sit on my lap which resulted in a considerable amount of disruption.

The goats huffed and puffed their way to the top like the rest of us, Samantha grumping at this demand made upon her and complaining when we urged her on each time she showed a preference to pause and graze. While the two groups of musterers made their ways north and south, those of us at the catching pen cut scrub and, by weaving the branches through the wire, managed to camouflage the netting and rearrange the landscape. We crawled on hands and knees searching for any glint of wire that might alert the goats to a trap — if and when they got them that far. Then we waited for the first crackle to come through the walkie-talkie.

The warm sun and spectacular view overlooking the strait helped ease the tension. Everyone came alive at the first barkings of the dogs, still some distance away. We could see nothing, but the excited sounds of the dogs made it clear the muster had begun. We could only watch and wait.

Mike searched the shimmering cliffs with his binoculars for any sign of activity. The sun reflecting on the waters of the strait turned our view to the north into a blur of moving light and it was some time before he could distinguish the figures of men and women outlined on the distant cliffs. A herd of goats ran swiftly and surefootedly in front of them, their flight spurred on by the barkings of the dogs and the whistles and shouts of the volunteers.

'Here they come.' Mike said calmly, and I foolishly jumped to my feet.

Someone wisely pulled me back to cover and, with everyone whispering directions, we crept to the edge of the ridge where we could now see the goats approaching along the low track. We held our breaths as they moved past us, hoping they would not decide to come up, but would continue along the bottom. They did, passing over the netting lying on the ground. Mike radioed the party waiting around the next ridge that the goats were coming and when they disappeared from sight, we sprang into action.

Men scrambled down the cliffs, ropes around their waists for safety, and attached the netting to the waiting posts, then scrub was lowered to them and inserted into the fence. It all had to be done quickly for we had no idea how the goats would react when they came face to face with the waiting musterers.

Mitch stayed at the bottom with his dog to keep the goats from running below while the rest hauled themselves to the top and we took up our prearranged positions around the catching pen.

'Okay, we're ready!' Mike whispered into the handset, and the goats were headed back towards the newly-erected fence line.

It was a tense half-hour as we waited to see if the plan would work. The goats were wary and in their anxiety had picked up momentum, retracing their steps until they came to the fence that had appeared since they passed over the track moments before. They milled about assessing the situation, aware of the men and dogs ahead and coming up from behind. Sniffing the air, they became aware, too, of Mitch and Tipua below them. If they didn't bolt and try to break through the line of musterers, there was a good chance they would seek escape by the one unobstructed route left to them; and this they did, heading up in our direction.

Samantha and Jody were prodded into position and tied where they would be seen by the goats as they topped the ridge, but when I attempted to leave them, they cried out in alarm and, fearing their anxious bleatings might have a deterring rather than a beckoning effect on the approaching herd, I crammed myself under a manuka bush, trying to be as invisible as possible. No-one spoke or moved and, from my vantage point near the entrance to the catching pen, I saw the horns and ears of the first goats appear over the ridge.

'Jody!' I called softly and she obligingly answered loudly enough to attract the advance guard which turned in her direction and led the rest of the herd into the enclosure.

I stayed frozen and, from my place under the manuka, witnessed the most amazing panorama of legs, flying feet, dogs and goats whizzing by oblivious of my presence. How I avoided being trampled by men's heavy boots, bitten by snapping dogs or caught on the big bucks' flaying horns is a wonder, for once the goats realised the trick played upon them, they raced about in panic, searching for an escape.

Many piled up in one corner of the pen and there were fearful screams from those caught in the crush.

The volunteers dived into the seething mass and hauled the largest ones away, trussing and tranquilising them, allowing air and space for those caught in the front and preventing any smothering of the smaller animals.

The remainder of the volunteers had by now all converged at the pen and kept any avenues of escape closed to the goats. All this I observed from the shelter of the manuka as every attempt I made to dislodge myself met with a flurry of dogs, boots and goats, necessitating a hasty retreat.

Samantha and Jody had worked themselves into a frenzy and had wound the restraining ropes tightly around the surrounding bushes as the drama raged around them. I finally managed to release them and rushed to help the others, but they had the situation well under control by the time I joined them.

It is difficult to describe the next step in this rescue, for it was of such monumental proportions words seem inadequate. Each of the goats had to be carried down the ridge to the waiting boat. The path was long and steep, but all 114 goats were carried, one at a time, the men back-packing the bucks, while the women carried the smaller does.

As we laboured up and down the ridge there were moments of laughter as the men with bucks on their backs approached. The legs of the animals had been tied so that the men could slip the goats on like a jacket, producing the illusion of a two-headed apparition, the buck's head above the carrier, his beard flowing over the head of the man. This was especially comical when the man carrying the goat had little or no hair of his own and suddenly was blessed with an instant 'toupee' of billy-goat beard. Many made several trips for animals and everyone worked so very hard that day. The heat was intense and the ordeal very taxing for man and animal alike.

As I arrived on the beach after my second trip, I found Yvonne and some of the other women bending over a doe suffering from the heat and stress. We ran to the sea for water and one of the women tore her skirt to provide rag for sponging the doe, whose body was feverish and panting. Loving hands held water for her to drink as others gently wiped her body with the cooling water. Slowly she responded and we placed her under a tree where she rested and recovered much to our relief.

Up and down we trudged, bringing down each time a struggling animal, wondering if we would have the strength for another trip, feeling certain we would not. Tempers flared in the heat, provoked by the physical stress we were under. Questions were raised as to the future of the goats on Aotea. What, some demanded, did we plan to do in years to come when the population exploded and feed was short? They had not come all this way and worked so hard to see the animals starve to death.

Others felt there were too many bucks and that some decision should be made about their future. One faction advocated shooting them cleanly and quickly now, while others wanted to let them go and take their chances with the Forest Service shooters.

People questioned each other's motives and angry words were spoken. It was a wave of human emotion, reactions brought on by strain and exhaustion, but through it all the goats were brought to safety and taken by launch to Aotea.

In order to keep the goats on Aotea, we had to earmark and tag each one and the screams of the animals as they were held and tagged caused the more tender-hearted to flinch in horror. Celia's gentle heart broke at the cries and many walked away in disgust, but it had to be done, such was the law. It was a distasteful job, but if we wanted to keep the goats on Aotea as anything other than feral animals, they had to be branded. Those who performed the operation were scorned and ridiculed by some who thought it cruel and it caused a great deal of dissension as did the debate over the supposed excess of bucks. Everyone came to me for final decisions which I was incapable of making due to fatigue, and bewilderment with the varying opinions and personalities.

The last of the goats were loaded on to the boats and taken to East Bay and released within the confines of the electric fence. I chose not to accompany the expedition, feeling it should be a New Zealand exercise. Instead I walked out along the track and watched as the goats were unloaded. In groups of two and three they made their way to the safe hills of Aotea. Tears of gratitude blurred my vision; gratitude to the many men and women who had given so much over the years to save the animals I cared about so deeply. Few people know of the efforts of those people or what they accomplished; their reward came from within, the satisfaction of a job well done and perhaps one to be appreciated by posterity.

Unsung heroes and heroines from all walks of New Zealand life had come in answer to the call of the animals and had helped to blaze a new path in the field of conservation. Together we had done all we could do to create a sanctuary on Aotea, for many of us believed then, as now, that the Arapawa goat belonged on the island to which it had adapted so well over two centuries.

CHAPTER X

A Time To Weep

The day had begun like so many others at Aotea . . . with a crisis. In fact, several of them. Walt had returned to his bed overcome by the effects of a severe case of boils, a malady that had begun at Te Anau and had plagued him through Pelorus Sound to Aotea. Over the years he was to play host to hundreds of the things, ranging in size from pimples to full-fledged carbuncles. Unfortunately, a goodly number had chosen his posterior upon which to reside and that resulted in some extremely unhappy days in the saddle, plus many a stand-up dinner. He had been treated with every known medical remedy and an equal number of homegrown cures that included the tortures of placing the mouth of a boiled milk bottle over the boil in an attempt to 'pop' it to the more gentle treatment of gin and nutmeg. Just what the curative properties of this oft-recommended concoction were, we could not discover, and although it did nothing to halt the outbreak of boils, it did allow Walt to sleep though some of the more chronic stages.

Extra mashed potatoes were prepared with dinner and applied to the various parts of Walt's anatomy. Sometimes the potatoes were mixed with honey and yoghurt in an effort to do for Walt what such an application had done for Billy Jo. We soaked him in salt water and encased his body in boiled dock leaves. He tried fasting and feasting on diets ranging from raw foods to only grapes. The 'Grape Diet' promised a magical cure and Walt would have happily lain in his bed popping grapes like a languid, carbuncled Caesar, had the promise included the magical dollars needed for the kilos of grapes meant to be consumed. Not only was payment a problem, but procurement as well. No-one, it seemed, stocked the quantities of the succulent fruit necessary to effect a cure and before we came to the conclusion that grapes were a remedy we could neither obtain nor afford, we stripped Picton bare of every purple cluster.

Having resorted to more conventional means, Walt was, on this particular day, undergoing the treatment of being mummified in steamed lily leaves from the waist down and he lay in abject misery as the poison in his system caused his temperature to rise to an uncomfortable fever.

To add to our woes, the toilet had refused to flush for several days and all that could be squeezed from the water taps was mud and the occasional worm which indicated problems at the reservoir.

Bertha chose this time to be particularly perverse and belched us out of the kitchen which she filled with smoke. With Mary and Roy away and Walt in no condition to assist, I attached Bertha from the chimney down while Mitch trudged up the hill to our water supply to ascertain the trouble.

'It's big trouble, Mom,' he announced cheerfully. 'The filter's gone and the hose is clogged, all 100 metres of it!'

He sounded like he wanted help, but since I had both arms down Bertha's throat brushing her tonsils, I could only wish him luck.

Some hours later, having attacked Bertha from without and within, I backed away from my rebellious relic and surveyed the scene. Bertha had done to the kitchen from ceiling to floor what she had done to me from head to toe; covered us both with a residue of black soot, the removal of which would require very hot, soapy water.

Heading for the creek, the only source of clean water — in fact, the only source of any water — I passed the bathroom just as Malama, the cat, jumped through the open window with a large bird in her mouth. Dropping the bucket, I rushed to free the bird, which, thankfully, was not hurt, although understandably frightened. Malama was deposited outside and the bird, a banded pigeon, was put in a box to settle down.

Like Old Mother Hubbard, I found the woodbox quite bare when I prepared to stoke up Bertha. This was a job Walt usually took care of but his condition had sent him to bed instead of to the chopping block. I trotted back and forth with the wheelbarrow filling the woodbox as Mitch trotted up and down the hillside trying to dislodge mud.

Bertha, her arteries cleaned, purred like a kitten and obliged me by heating several buckets of water hauled from the creek. I dragged the table to the kitchen, placed a chair on top of it and, when the water was piping hot, climbed atop the pyramid and proceeded to scrub the ceiling. Rivulets of water ran down my arms and dripped on to my blackened face and clothing, leaving me striped, not unlike a zebra.

It was at this moment I heard a boat pull up at the jetty. I sagged from my perch, muttering that this was hardly the time for visitors, but acknowledging this was usually when we got them . . . when everything was in an uproar!

Mitch came in the back door, weary and dejected, and announced what I already knew — the hose was still clogged, for the taps in the bath had greeted me with loud sucking gasps when I tried for a quick wash-up to make myself more presentable for our unexpected guests. Having armed himself with every conceivable tool, Mitch managed one free hand into which I placed the pigeon with instructions to release it when he was far away from the house.

Our visitors were still busy tying themselves in knots on the jetty, a sure sign they were 'day-trippers or weekenders' and I made use of the delay to scramble to the creek with a bar of soap, but the cold water only succeeded in rearranging the smudge and left me anything but presentable. Looking like a begrimed street urchin, I greeted our guests, apologising for my appearance with explanations of the difficulties we were experiencing with the wood stove. However, Leroy, a small child encased in an overly large life jacket, had no time for explanations or apologies for his was the need that brought them from their fishing in the bay . . . he desperately needed to use the toilet. Why couldn't they have wanted to use the telephone? Now I politely explained we were having difficulties in that area as well and had been using a bucket for our most intimate needs for the last few days.

By now, Leroy was dancing up and down inside his life jacket and Mama said a bucket would do fine. Why he couldn't use a bush was beyond me. I ushered them into the house, trying to divert their attention from the bedroom door through which Walt could be seen dozing like a great green giant, on to the bathroom where I indicated the bucket. Leroy demanded privacy and before Mama, Daddy and I stepped into the passage, I suggested they remove the life jacket as there seemed no possible way for Leroy to assume a sitting position encased as he was, whereupon Leroy displayed all the symptoms of a child tyrant, something akin to Caligula. Promising their little darling everything under the sun to compensate for the removal of the jacket, while Leroy displayed an amazing aptitude for child-power, we finally relieved him of his encumbrance. Leroy was enthroned on the bucket and we were dismissed to wait in the corridor until beckoned; and beckoned we were by such piercing screams that we nearly fell over one another getting through the door.

The cause of Leroy's hysteria was Malama who had come through the window with the same pigeon in his mouth and was endeavouring to present it to Leroy. The poor pigeon must have been completely shell-shocked, placed as it was between Malama's jaws and Leroy's screaming face, and it's a wonder the bird didn't have a heart attack on the spot. Mama rescued Leroy while I rescued the pigeon, placing it once more in the box. Again we stepped discreetly into the passage and again Leroy screamed. Malama had been unceremoniously dumped out the front door and had strolled around to the window, jumped in and was sitting on Leroy's lap rubbing her head under his chin, oblivious to his screaming protests.

Leroy, Mama explained, was terrified of cats; I, in turn, was terrified Leroy was going to have a major accident with the bucket as he teetered left and right in an effort to remove Malama. Daddy grabbed the bucket, Mama grabbed Leroy and I scooped up Malama, depositing her in the bedroom to avoid any further contact, wondering if Leroy was ever going to do what he so urgently came to do and I was greatly relieved when he did and they left. I later discovered the dear child had put the entire roll of toilet paper, our last one, in the bucket.

With that charming interlude out of the way, I returned to the kitchen. By now all my hot water had cooled. Setting the buckets on the stove to reheat, I fixed Walt some light lunch and checked his progress. We had no sooner decided the best place for Walt was in bed when Mitch arrived with further tales of woe — the hose was unclogged but we now had an airlock and he had come to Walt for advice. Walt was consulted and with great effort rose from his bed of lily leaves and limped feverishly to the rescue. Mitch was again handed the pigeon to take further than the furthest point possible on his return trip to the reservoir, and I resumed the task of cleaning the kitchen.

'Oh, no!' came the anguished cry from the direction of the top shed and I rapidly made the descent from chair to table to floor and, looking out the window, saw a fountain of water resembling Old Faithful gushing from the pipes that wound their way around the shed.

First, the good news — the airlock was broken. Next, the bad news — the water, instead of flowing through the normal channels, had headed en masse for the shed and the pipe, ancient and rusty, could not take the sudden rush and had burst.

The ruptured pipe lay behind a thick fringe of stinging nettle, a prickly plant capable of inflicting a painful sting on even slight contact, and the men began slashing and pulling at the obstacle. As they slogged on, the geyser, spouting well above the roof top, poured quantities of water and mud all over them and turned the area into a quagmire; the mud gripping their boots like partially hardened cement when they tried to move on. They floundered and fell, unable at times to avoid the angry sting of the nettle, caught in their own little cloudburst on an otherwise cloudless day. I winced each time Walt fell, knowing the pain it must be causing his boils and admired his tenacity and spirit.

The light had left the sky before the men were able to bring the situation under control, by which time Walt was well spent. Mitch, equally battle-scarred, apologised profusely for causing Walt to leave his sick bed, but obviously the enormity of the problem was such that Mitch could not have been expected to cope alone.

I had been struggling, not with geysers, but with buckets and rivulets and had managed in a stop-start fashion to complete the cleaning of the kitchen and all that it contained. Although the water was now flowing to the house, it had not had time to course through Bertha's wetback and produce the hot showers we all desperately needed, so we heated enough on Bertha's top to rid ourselves of all but the most ground-in dirt, gathered dock leaves for our toilet needs and after a very quick meal, crawled wearily between the sheets.

My head hadn't hit the pillow before I heard that special 'meow' Malama uses to announce she has successfully gone a-hunting and reluctantly I left my bed and shuffled to the bathroom to find Malama, for the third time, holding the pigeon and casting about for someone to give it to. Our persistent cat happily handed over the perplexed pigeon who by now, must have been thoroughly benumbed by Malama's insistence, and who remained in the safe box throughout the night without so much as a rustle of feathers.

By contrast, Mike, our Silky terrier, was extremely vocal. He choked and wheezed through the night in such obvious distress, that any hope of sleep, no matter how badly sought after, was cancelled.

Dawn found Walt, Mike, pigeon and I ready to leave for town and the vet. Two hours later found us still sitting there as Walt laboured with the motor that refused to start. Mike wheezed and I wailed that Walt must do something, for Mike was surely dying. Walt was, of course, doing everything in his power to correct the situation and finally the *Aotea* chugged into life. We made it to Picton by nine and drove hurriedly to Blenheim, my little friend almost lifeless and gasping in my arms. I rushed tearfully into the surgery and, as we laid him down in preparation for an examination, Mike gave one huge hacking cough and deposited a piece of bone neatly on the gleaming stainless steel table. He immediately stopped dying and gasping and was, in fact, very much alive and well! Our relief for Mike was immense, but how we wished he could have performed the regurgitation act some time earlier. Just to be certain we would have not to make a second trip to town on Mike's behalf, the vet anaesthetised him and checked his windpipe for any damage, then pronounced him fit to return home.

No longer gasping, Mike was now flopping in my arms like a miniature drunk with no coordination or control as he fought the after-effects of the drug. I sat on the back of the boat shading him from the sun, watching Walt, sweating and weary, struggling to coax the boat into life for the journey home. She seemed to be suffering from the same malady that had seized her at dawn and when the cause had finally been determined, Walt announced we had indeed been lucky to have ever made it to Picton. A new part was procured and, after much clanging of spanners and turning of screws, we headed for home, the sunset at our backs.

Before we left the vet, we had handed over the pigeon and asked if he would find its owner through the local pigeon club. We later learned the bird had been destroyed because it had flown off course. The poor creature had survived Malama's persistent attentions only to become pigeon pie due to a faulty compass.

On the trip home, I reflected on the last 48 hours that had seen us lurching from crisis to crisis, devoid of sleep and running at fever pitch. Any one event of the previous two days was enough to have tested our resolve and ability to cope, yet fate had a way of conspiring against us at times, wearing us thin, then coming in for the body blow. I wondered if everyone who lived as we did had the same problems. Had we chosen a way of life ill-suited to our capabilities and style or were we being tested, forever tested?

To Walt's more practical mind, the events were nothing more than daily challenges to be met and overcome, then forgotten when his head hit the pillow, but my fanciful, always-looking-for-meanings mind saw all the signs of a gauntlet flung.

The family in the States had counselled us against leaving the security of home and hearth and predicted that we'd be back in the 'good ole U.S.A.' within six months. Another six months had been granted by some of our New Zealand associates when we headed for Aotea. Both of these deadlines had come and gone, but I had to confess we had hung in there at times by the skin of our teeth and something very akin to pride, hiding any vulnerability and insecurity behind the veneer of a tough, pioneering spirit. Things hadn't turned out as I had expected, not yet anyway. Maybe we just needed more time.

We didn't get it. Like the dance of so many devils, Old Man Southerly fell upon us with even more of a vengeance than we had come to anticipate. The sky darkened and the wind whipped the water into maddened, whirling dervishes across the bay to splatter themselves against our big doors. Ocean-sized waves crashed over the jetty and *Aotea* struggled against her ropes like a wild horse when first saddled. We watched as the dinghy, which had been securely tied and burdened with extra weight, became airborne and sailed across the bay, landing limp and shattered. Glass in the greenhouse split, then tinkled to the ground and I drew the curtain lest the same fate awaited our ranch-slider doors.

With a wrench and a sickly rasping sound, the Old Man tore the roof from the hen-house and dug it deep into the hillside above the homestead. Trees fell like matchsticks, one large ancient monarch narrowly missing the house. I had been at the kitchen sink when I heard the crack and watched transfixed as the roots were sucked from the earth, the dark shape towering above me like a huge black giant mortally wounded before he fell. I ran from the kitchen as it hurtled to the ground, shaking the house to its foundations, its branches scraping and clawing at the window. The mound of earth it uprooted stood well over my head and had it struck the house we would have been minus most of our kitchen and Bertha would have been but a memory.

Now the heavens poured out oceans of water, so much so that the placid creeks turned into raging torrents, spilling over banks and running through the garden. My tenderly nurtured cluster of herbs was no longer recognisable and all in the garden lay battered and sodden.

The water that ran through the taps was the colour of old beer and had the consistency of thick malt as once again the filter was ripped away and the hose was twisted like spaghetti on a fork. Fences were washed away and all the lovely sparkling streams that dot the hillsides became angry thundering cascades, slashing to the beach and convulsing themselves into the sea.

During the height of the storm, the roof of the woolshed lifted ominously and showed every indication of joining the henhouse roof arrowed in on the hill. Mitch volunteered to climb out and drive some nails to hold it until the storm abated and it could be properly repaired. With a rope around his waist and Walt on the other end, he slipped from the window of the top shed and climbed to the peak, inching his way to the corner of the woolshed roof overhanging the sea.

Descending was hazardous; the rain had made the roofing iron slippery and it pitched towards the sea where jagged rocks jutted through the water. The wind buffeted his body and whipped the rain about his face. Our greatest fear was that the iron would rip away and become airborne, turning it into a guillotine with Mitch defenceless in its path. As Mitch moved closer the Old Man taunted us by wrenching yet another nail from the roof. Then Mitch slipped and, clutching and clawing at the roof, began to slide slowly to the edge. Walt heaved with all his strength in response to the pull on the rope and I hid my face in my hands.

When I dared to look again, Mitch was gripping the peak of the roof with his toes, heading face downward, hammering his way to the very edge, plunging mushroom-headed nails into the resisting roof. He won the battle and was hauled head over heels through the window to safety.

Maybe, I thought, this is what it's all about — winning battles, not being beaten, picking up the pieces and starting over again. It took nearly a week to restore some semblance of order; the damage to fences and paddocks being given lesser priority than the immediate vicinity of the homestead.

The past few weeks had been a miniature kaleidoscope of what getting away from it all had been like ever since we had embarked on the adventure several years before. In the search for peace and quiet we had chosen isolation and substituted new problems and challenges for other, less demanding ones.

Lesson One — Isolation does not automatically equate with peace and tranquility, and getting away from it all can mean getting into the thick of it.

Lesson Two — One does not gracefully or easily adapt to the physical and emotional demands such a drastic change in life style brings, for from a life of apparent ease, indulgence and dependency, we had flung ourselves into a reverse situation. Everything was now labour-intensive and even simple reflex actions took on a new dimension. For instance, it was now possible to flick the switch for light but such a little thing required moments of reflection and decision-making. The 'genny' burned fuel, could we afford it? Could I manage in the twilight zone of half-light or did my needs justify the use of precious diesel and the accompanying noise?

And there were a few other things that were making life on our island paradise less than idyllic. Preparing meals, whether in the eye-straining dimness or by guilt-producing light, required many hours. Vegetables had to be dug, pulled or picked and in most cases came with quantities of attached dirt. Prudently, the clods of clinging earth had to be returned to the garden and all inedible leaves, pods, skins or shells deposited in the compost. For the flesh-eaters of the family, fish had to be caught, mutton mustered or pig stalked, then skinned, hung, cut, cooked and finally eaten.

Milk did not pour from a bottle, it had to be obtained from our cow and goats — twice a day, rain or shine. Buckets and utensils had to be sterilised, the animals fed, watered and kept in clean, dry conditions. Sacks of barley and bales of hay had to be lugged from boat to shed to feed these producers of fresh milk which was made into yoghurt, butter and cheese, all time-consuming tasks. Eggs involved a search-and-find operation and the poultry had to be fed twice daily and their housing kept clean and odourless. Every spare moment was devoted to making bread with enough to spare should unexpected guests arrive.

With all that we had very little time for the unscheduled or unexpected, but both those variations were becoming so frequent that I decided we would have to forget about a schedule altogether and just roll with the punches. Basically, that was what we had been doing anyway — taking each hectic day as it presented itself — but we had been kidding ourselves that ours was a ship-shape, well-run organisation!

We were not moulding our destinies, rather were we reacting, knee-jerk fashion, to the daily crises that seemed to have no end. Over and over I told myself, once we get the plumbing sorted out, or Bertha gets an extension to her chimney, or once the fence line is completed, or one of the hundred other jobs demanding our attention was finished, then things would settle down, but deep in my heart, I kept thinking of the gauntlet.

Walt, a plodder at heart, marched steadfastly through each non-conforming day, taking things as they came. Outwardly I coped; inwardly I nurtured a growing resentment that the days, weeks, months were being eaten away by sheer drudgery. Reading, the joy of my life, was almost a forgotten pleasure, quiet walks in the woods, few and far between, time with the animals diminished to stolen moments.

I seemed to be faced with stacks — stacks of dishes, stacks of

A soon to be safe, but none the less puzzled and unhappy Arapawa doe awaits her turn to be taken to safety. Note the hobble designed to restrain the animal with a minimum of stress.

Nestled among the trees the "heap of rubble" we transformed into a home.

The look in Walt's eye as he contemplates a serious matter is not unlike his expression when he learned he was to become the instant grandfather of Richard 5, Rachael 3 and Loren 1.

letters, stacks of dirty laundry. Outbuildings waited to be cleaned, milk to be made into yoghurt and cheese, layers of Bertha's grimy indiscretions to be repeatedly scrubbed away. In short, I was overwhelmed by the sheer enormity of self-sufficiency and much of the joy had gone from my life.

As if I hadn't enough to cope with, I'd given myself the added burden of sparring with the Knowledgables, a full-time job on its own. I felt hemmed in, captive and depressed, and spent valuable time taking to my bed, nursing my self-pity and a touch of the vapours.

Walt had enough on his plate to prevent his noticing, much less sharing, my dilemma and I languished, exhausted and spent. The 'Me' of yesteryear sat petite, polished, pampered and smug on the edge of my bed surveying the 'Me' of today that had got away from it all — pudgy, bedraggled, overworked and hating every self-sufficient minute.

'Well, Betty,' said my Spirit of Christmas Past, 'isn't this what you wanted?'

She took one of my hardened, leathery hands with permanently black-ringed fingernails into her own soft ones.

'Been washing your clothes in black streams, I see!' she mocked me.

I snatched my hand away and hid under the covers, sobbing. I cried myself to sleep dreaming of my elegant house in Richboro with every conceivable appliance at my fingertips. I'd had much more time before, time to do things I could barely spare a thought for now. I used to read four books a week and walk seven miles a day, no matter what the weather.

The shop in the village had delivered the groceries and dinner was usually an effortless transition from freezer to table after which the dishwasher took over. No heavy-laden trips to the compost; the garbage disposal gobbled up all the leftovers. The washer and dryer kept our fashionable clothing neat and clean and I paid to have the ironing done once a fortnight. My own car whizzed me wherever I wanted to go and I could take long, soaking baths three times a day if I felt like it. The toilet always flushed and I didn't have to agonise every time I turned on a light.

Now here I was on some God-forsaken island, working from 5.30 a.m. till 10 at night, seven days a week. I'd almost forgotten how to read and considered myself fortunate to take a quick shower every third day. My clothing, which I once chose with great care and flair, now consisted of second-hand, tattered misfits, usually caked with mud and muck, which I wore until I felt compelled to change on purely hygienic grounds.

If we weren't battening down for or cleaning up after Old Man Southerly, we were digging, planting, grubbing, fencing, building, repairing, mustering, dipping, milking, cleaning, stoking, chopping. Something had gone wrong, terribly wrong. It all seemed insurmountable and unbearable, and suddenly I hated it. Hated going without a shower for a week because there was no water, despised Bertha for the extra work she made, shuddered and shivered as I poked my posterior into a bush on a cold, wet night when the toilet refused to flush, fumed when the men dumped layers of begrimed work clothes on the waiting pile of laundry. The beauty and the rapture were gone and I wallowed in the greyness of discontent.

Although I have little else to thank the then Minister of Lands and Forests for, I owe him my gratitude for helping me find my way out of a very depressed state of mind. Of the many letters I felt obliged to write, one had been an 18-page handwritten epistle endeavouring to explain in detail the case concerning the Arapawa wildlife. I had laboured long and hard over that letter and almost had to pry the pen from my fingers when I finally signed it. Eighteen pages of longhand constitutes an enormous amount of writing and I exploded with indignation when I received a terse two paragraphs in reply. The Minister's ears must have flamed into crimson and bells exploded in his head with the expletives I showered on him from afar!

I determined on the spot that my efforts on behalf of the animals would not cease because of the growing weariness in my forearm and I would not become a slave to the ballpoint, indeed I would not become a slave to anything. I went straight to the telephone and rang Mary asking if she was using her typewriter. She was not and yes, she would send it out on the next mailboat. I did not know how to type, but vowed I would learn and, armed with ink erasers and Twink, I did just that. The results for me were fantastic. Hours spent writing to family, friends and Knowledgables were now reduced by a third! Another phone call alleviated the bread problem and now the shop sent four loaves a week, leaving me the pleasure of making it when and if I so chose.

One of the major changes made as I picked up the gauntlet was to set aside for myself part of each day to do whatever I wanted — a walk, reading, resting, yoga, watching the animals — and I refused to let myself or anyone else make me feel guilty about it. My anger at the impertinence of Big Brother had acted as a safety valve allowing me to let off the steam of pent-up frustration rather than hide from the problems that beset me.

Self-sufficiency can mean self-destruction, I reasoned, if I determined to do for myself all that society with its various servicing industries had previously done for me. Each of the tasks I had assigned myself were time- and energy-consuming and most were required to be performed daily. Thus I had planned my days around them allowing for little flexibility. The constant interruptions had thrown any semblance of order to the wind until unfinished chores had piled high about me.

The responsibility of keeping in touch with loved ones had forced me to write numerous repetitive letters striving to pour love and a sense of intimacy into each one. Anything less than two pages made me feel guilty and insensitive to those we left behind. The duplicated letter dilemma was solved by typing three copies of the same general information and filling in the 'Dear So and So' with any personal comments at a later date.

Photographs were sent with a request to see they were circulated amongst family and friends and then returned. Varying the contents of the photo packets, we were able to share more of our life at Aotea by shuffling the packets from one interested group to another. It saved time and money, for not only was I photographing events at Aotea, but I was now snapping pictures of the Arapawa goats from all angles and in all circumstances and sending these overseas, mainly to one Mr A.R. Werner. An historian, specialising in agricultural history, he had written requesting a photograph of an Arapawa buck and from this request sprang a long and fruitful correspondence. On receiving the several photos I supplied, Mr Werner replied: 'The photographs of the Arapawa goat were, in my opinion, of stock almost indistinguishable from the original English breed'.

I was overjoyed, for Mr Werner had to his credit numerous research papers on rare and primitive breeds and was involved in the efforts to reconstitute the English goat in Britain. He made a concise, intelligent submission to the Marlborough Sounds Maritime Park Board which was read scornfully by the chairman and totally ignored by the board. The board, it seemed, preferred to take its advice from Knowledgables who came up with such intelligent and perceptive suggestions as declaring the goats to be no more 'old scrubbers and useless', then advocating the expenditure of taxpayers' money to 'preserve the gene pool of the Arapawa goats'!

The aim of all my rearranging and priority setting was to bring the sunshine back into my life. We were surrounded by beauty, wild and savage at times, gentle and exquisite at others. I was determined to enjoy, absorb and learn from it. I was not going to spend all my time scurrying around being everything from chimney sweep and milkmaid to chief cook and bottle-washer. No, I had not travelled 10,000 miles for a change of sinks, nor to set myself unobtainable goals. There is a time for everything and I had to see to it that the precious moments needed for personal growth and rejuvenation were provided and that a glorious sunset did not fade from the sky unnoticed because I was too preoccupied. I could not permit the Knowledgables to invade my life with their inane utterances. I had had my time to weep, now it was time to fight.

CHAPTER XI

The Protest

'The bastards are here!' The words pierced through the telephone to my heart. The day we had fought, argued, lobbied and struggled against had arrived. 'They've landed by helicopter. We can hear the shooting.'

I felt a stunned anguish, then a well of tears burst into racking sobs. I stumbled to the woolshed where the men were shearing to tell them the Forest Service had landed and had come out shooting.

'We've got to do something!' I sobbed.

Walt nodded, left the shed and went to the boat to prepare her for the trip to East Bay.

Celia and Sid, the English couple now living with us permanently, had come to Aotea when the job they had held as caretakers for a wealthy landowner had become untenable and they had felt compelled to leave. They were as committed to the preservation of the Arapawa wildlife as we were and had, prior to coming to Aotea, received a phone call warning them not to get involved with us or support us in the fight. It took courage to ignore the warning, for by now the situation had become one of ever-lowering levels of personal abuse and acrimony.

Our chance encounter with the Wigmores arose over a pair of geese and evolved into a friendship of great depth and understanding. Celia and Sid left England for many of the same reasons that we had left the States — in search of the quiet, uncomplicated life of self-sufficiency, and found themselves living not far from us in the Sounds. They had launched wholeheartedly into all the accepted ways of providing for themselves — chickens, goats, gardens, etc — and had decided the next addition should be geese. About the same time I had come to a similar conclusion for Aotea.

After an unsuccessful attempt to capture some surplus geese in Tory Channel, I planned to place an advertisement in the paper. Celia beat me to it. When I read her advertisement, I frugally thought to save myself the expensee of placing my own and rang the number to see how she had fared. Once the formalities and her lack of success had

133

been discussed, we tentatively questioned one another and in the lengthy conversation that followed, found we had much in common. Celia and Sid certainly could have fostered more rewarding friendships as they took up life in New Zealand, for our relationship embroiled them almost as deeply in the wildlife battle as ourselves and if ever a friendship was forged out of love, sharing and mutual agony, it was ours.

Not long after we met, Celia was travelling the Knowledgable circuit with me. Poised, dignified and with cool English charm, she was a perfect foil for my outspoken, brash, direct attacks on bureaucracy. While I thumped on pulpits and hopped from one soapbox to another, Celia arranged schedules, packed bags, sorted my papers and got me to where I was going on time. She coaxed, cajoled, commiserated and rebuked when necessary and bolstered my failing courage when I wanted to turn tail and run.

This unlikely mentor, whose English reserve had prevented her speaking to strangers, soon became as adept as I in narrating the story of the Arapawas. Together we took on Big Brother, stood before a select committee of parliamentarians and faced television crews, talkback programmes and lengthy newspaper interviews. We grappled with Ministers of the Crown, braved the freezing wind and rain on Conservation Day to extol the virtues of the Old English goat and, in the Christchurch Town Hall, addressed an austere gathering of the International Union for the Conservation of Nature and Natural Resources.

Celia became an executive member of the Arapawa Wildlife Preservation Trust and later assumed the position of Research Officer. She and Sid were to remain with us at Aotea for a year and joined the ranks of those whose lives became intertwined with those of the Arapawa goats.

Ashley and Yvonne, among the first to answer the call of the Arapawas, had joined us on the island. It has been a source of great wonder to me that from the tragedy of the Arapawa wildlife has come so much that is beautiful and good — so many people it has been a privilege to know, so many friendships we would never have made otherwise.

Ashley and Yvonne had come to love the island through their experiences with the wildlife and were, in time, able to purchase land bordering ours in East Bay; they were now our neighbours. They brought with them their great capacity for love and life and, as landowners, could exert more influence on the fate of the wildlife.

Now we were all faced with the arrival of the shooters, an event each of us had fought so strenuously to prevent. Our first reaction was one of confusion. We had not made any plans for a protest, simply because all intelligent reasoning had indicated the threats to kill the wildlife were unreal. Numerous departmental reports had singled the goats out as special, although stopping short of agreeing with us on their Old English origins. Time and again those disagreeing with me publicly had privately urged me to keep fighting and said they would do what they could behind the scenes. The possibility that the Minister would allow the Park Board to carry out their extermination plan and wantonly destroy a rare and primitive breed was unthinkable. But complacency is never an attitude to be assumed when differing with bureaucracy, nor should anyone believe that sweet, intelligent reason will prevail; these assumptions can be fatal and indeed they were for the goats.

Much to the surprise of the Forest Service squad, who I do not believe anticipated any interference of a physical nature, Walt, Ashley, Yvonne and Mark, a young man who had been involved with the last two musters of the goats, appeared on the horizon.

The unsuspecting animals on the ridge had been easy targets for the shooters, but others had fled after the first frightening volleys echoed across the hilltops. In an effort to divert the goats from the line of fire, Walt and the others dislodged rocks and sent them cascading down the hill creating a commotion that caused hunter and hunted alike to seek safety elsewhere. The shooters headed for their camp and the goats ran for cover.

While Walt, Ashley, Yvonne and Mark did their best to disrupt the initial actions of the shooters, Celia and I were frantically ringing Arthur Adcock and Ken Crisp, the other two members of the Wildlife Trust executive, to tell them what was happening. We also rang friends, newspapers, radio stations, anyone who might be concerned and able to exert some influence. Everyone's reaction was the same — disbelief, anger, frustration and a determination to 'do something', although just what any of us could do wasn't quite clear.

I told Arthur that already some of our people were on the hill, but, of course, I had no way of knowing if they had made contact with the shooters. Arthur said that he knew several people who would be pleased to come to our assistance. He would organise it.

The protest wasn't planned, it just happened. Conceived in rage and anger and nurtured by frustration and disbelief, the drama unfolded. It is not an easy thing to defy authority. A battle of words is one thing; lining up against an armed opposition that has the blessing of the government is quite another. However unfair the odds, I don't believe the Forest Service was totally comfortable or confident at the prospect of our physical presence. This became evident the following day, when our advance guard of four were waiting as the shooters emerged from their tents, and saw the looks of surprise and alarm their presence generated.

The man in charge, whom we privately christened 'The Rooster', radioed his superiors with the news that 'Mr Rowe, Mr and Mrs Gray and one other person were present and what should he do?'

The swearing reply from the other end came through loud and clear, followed by an order to a subordinate to 'get the chairman down to the island, FAST!'

The chairman did not make an appearance that day or any other day of the protest; instead he sent his secretary and a policeman, presumably for protection, to talk to 'these people'.

Walt was told that the protesters were not to obstruct the shooters and he, in turn, informed the authorities that he had every right to be in the reserve as no instructions to the contrary nor any warning of the operation had been issued.

The outcome of all this verbal muscle-flexing was that the shooters did not leave the camp due to the presence of 'civilians' and eventually the secretary and the law took to the air and returned to the mainland, no doubt satisfied they had frightened us with their display of authority.

I had not been able to disengage myself from the telephone which seemed to ring every five minutes. Newspapers I'd never heard of wanted a story, the radio wanted me to tape something for the morning's news report and Arthur was tearing out his hair trying to reach me with the latest on the volunteers leaving Christchurch for the island. It was a chaotic time trying to coordinate transportation, food requirements and keep the media happy, while longing to be with the others on the hill and know what was happening.

In the middle of it all, the mailboat arrived and leaning over the rail was a young man with a head full of ginger curls and a smile full of sunshine. 'Hi, Mrs Rowe, I'm Rob, remember?'

I stared at him blankly, my mind racing through the names and places I'd heard in the last few frantic days and then it clicked. A young man had written to us some time ago requesting a stay at Aotea to learn about organic farming and gardening. In the confusion I had completely forgotten that today was the agreed date for his arrival!

Without so much as a greeting, I warned: 'Rob, we are right in the middle of a protest over the goats and if you want to stay out of trouble, don't get off that boat!'

He smiled his glorious smile, swung down from the top deck, bringing his pack with him and gave me a great bear hug.

'Maybe you could use some help?' I loved him on the spot and once again a special someone came into our lives.

Celia and I eagerly pored over the letters and telegrams that arrived in the mailbag, sharing them with Rob who was trying to fathom exactly what was happening and why. To be truthful, I wasn't at all sure myself as to what was going on, except that people were disembarking bag and baggage from the water-taxi, all fired with indignation and ready to race up the hill to save the goats. Those who couldn't join us physically sent sacks of food; some even sent cheques to help finance our growing army of protesters. I was quite overcome by the response and overjoyed to find so many people cared.

Celia performed the impossible and somehow managed to feed us all. Sid kept Bertha chugging from dawn to dusk for she had 30 hungry, dirty protesters to feed and cleanse. Any army marches on its stomach they say, and without the combination of Celia and Bertha, we would have been a very hungry army indeed. Many thought I should stay at home and attend the phone, but I desperately wanted to join those who came to register their opposition and to be with the animals. Celia was left with the added burden of being public relations officer, as well as chief cook and bottle washer.

Ken arrived, exuding his particular blend of confidence and good humour. Ken had been with us for all the musters and was now almost a member of the family. Having shared in many of the zany happenings at Aotea, he was not at all surprised to arrive amidst chaos and confusion. While others might have looked on with disbelief, Ken had come to know that Aotea runs on a heartbeat that makes blood pressures rise. We had laughed until we cried at some of the improbable situations and made enough memories to last a lifetime. Now Ken was here to help us make more.

One memory I didn't want to live with was someone's injury or death because of their involvement with the protest. The worry that someone would be hurt consumed me. Those were real bullets being used by the shooters and, in the thick bush, an accident could so easily occur. As in the past, many who volunteered were not prepared for the steepness of the terrain where a fall could prove fatal. Though everyone assured me they were there of their own volition and I was in no way responsible, I carried the weight of any mishap fairly and squarely on my shoulders.

Thus, the day Rob failed to return with the others, I was nearly frantic with worry. Celia, Walt and I headed in one direction by boat, while another group climbed the hill to search for him. I have never known such immense relief as when he turned up safe and well. Just how I would ever explain an accident or death to the parents or spouse of a volunteer was something I couldn't even contemplate. Rob's overdue return served to heighten my anxiety and I realised what a deadly game we were playing.

Leaving Celia to deal with hearth and phone, and Sid helping Walt to keep the farm from coming to a complete halt, I climbed the hill on the third day, along with Yvonne, Ashley and Mark; Yvonne patiently keeping pace with me which meant we were soon left behind by the men. The other protesters, fresh and energetic, had gone ahead with Rob and Mitch as guides and were already shadowing the shooters. We could hear a few sporadic shots and Yvonne gripped my hand, her eyes misty with tears.

When we reached the top, Yvonne led the way into the bush along the ridge and we had gone but a short distance when she called softly to me: 'Betty, don't come this way. There are some dead ones here.'

Oh, dear God, I cried to myself, I'll never be able to stand this, but said aloud, 'I've got to see it sometime'. And I moved to her side.

There before us were a doe and her kid caught in death in a reclining position, their necks crossed in final embrace. Unseeing eyes stared glazed and shocked, and blood trickled from their mouths. I blinked away tears that fell on the lifeless bodies and knelt to stroke them, crushed by the weight of sadness. How beautiful they were, even in death and how utterly defenceless.

Ashley's voice called to us, harsh and bitter, 'Yvonne, Betty, you'd better come over here!'

I kissed the doe softly on her cheek and we turned and made our way to where Ashley and Mark stood, fists clenched, watching as one of the scientists gutted a freshly killed doe, the steam rising from the cavity that had moments before been her belly — a belly that had held the foetus now dangling from a large hook through its stomach as it was held aloft to be weighed. My throat filled with bile at the grotesque and grisly picture. The shooter stood silent and rigid, looking away into the distance above our heads; the scientist, busy with his weighing and sorting, never raised his eyes to meet ours.

I bent over the still warm, steaming body and ran my hands over the doe's side. 'I'm sorry, so very sorry,' I whispered and my heart broke.

I rose to my feet, shaking with impotent rage because there was nothing we could do to stop the terrible thing that was happening, and the words sprang from the depths of my being: 'You murderers, you bloody murderers!'

Giving no sign that he heard me, nor indicating any remorse, the scientist hacked the jaw from the doe and jammed it into a sack along with other pieces of its anatomy. Finally he rose to his feet and appraised us with cold eyes.

'That's the trouble with you, Mrs Rowe, you're too emotional.'

Emotional! If I had had something in my hand, I would have struck that man, for I've never known such an overwhelming feeling of horror and disgust. Only our weapons were words, and torrents of verbal abuse fell from our lips. There was no other way to express the outrage we were experiencing. We were not violent people but it took every ounce of control to keep from striking out in cold fury.

The scientist made a move towards a second dead goat not far from where we stood and I knew he would mutilate it as he had the one at our feet.

'Don't touch her. Don't you DARE touch her!'

Perhaps my voice sounded a warning? Perhaps they wearied of the interference? Whatever it was, they headed swiftly in the direction of the camp.

Before I left the house that morning, I had asked Celia to phone TVNZ and contact a journalist who had interviewed me after a talk I had given in Wellington. His parting words had been, 'If ever there is anything I can do to help, please let me know.'

'Tell him, Celia, that I am reminding him of his offer and we need him now.'

We had to let the country know what was happening.

By the time we reached the camp, the helicopter was hovering, camera crew on board, searching for a place to touch down in the rugged terrain. They interviewed three of us — a scientist, a shooter and me. We stated our various positions, the Forest Service claiming they were just there to do a job and had come in at the request of the Marlborough Sounds Maritime Park Board. The scientist they questioned, who had once been a friend of ours, claimed he was there to undertake a study — to determine if the shots fired at the goats would in any way disturb the wild sheep!

I bristled at the discrimination, and challenged him when we met later: 'Well, my friend, the moment of truth has arrived. Have you collected your 30 pieces yet?'

He protested that he hadn't wanted it to come to this and it was all upsetting him badly. I wasn't exactly on top of the world either. As he left the camp with a shooter, I called to him with all the bitterness I felt, 'Every time they shoot one, think of me!'

I knew it hurt and I didn't care. I wanted it to hurt, to make them feel guilty, to hurt them as they hurt the animals.

In order to deter the shooters and keep ourselves out of the line of fire, it was necessary for us to leave the Forest Service camp site when they did. This meant hauling weary bodies from sleeping bags at 4 a.m. Celia and Sid rose an hour earlier and stoked Bertha into life, packed lunches and prepared breakfast, after which we piled into *Aotea* and were taken to East Bay. Each day the 300-metre climb to the ridge grew more difficult and then there was the descent to the camp, hugging the shore on the Cook Strait side. By the time we reached the site, we had already been walking for several hours and very little of the ground we covered was level. Young and old legs alike rebelled, muscles throbbed, knees ached and breathing was done in short, sharp gasps. In the evening, we retraced our steps, climbing, always climbing.

We converged on the camp as the opposition were emerging from their tents. Yvonne usually gave them a cheery 'Good morning', although there was seldom any response other than a grunt or a cold, unwelcoming stare.

One morning, I arrived at the camp, last in line as usual, and stepped into the main tent in time to see cups of tea being poured. No offer was extended to us, so I announced that I'd like a cup too, please. In fact, we'd all (meaning the protesters) have a cup, thank you! A look of disdainful surprise crept over the face of the man holding the teapot.

'Getting a bit bossy, aren't you, Mrs Rowe?'

'As taxpayers, we provided that tea.' And I picked up a mug and held it to be filled. We sipped our tea while they ate their breakfast in sullen silence, doing their best to ignore our taunts and heckling.

We had watched them carefully, for some tried to slip away through the bushes without being detected and thus avoid another day of walking shoulder to shoulder with the protesters, or watching as their quarry was chased from the line of fire by shouts and yahooing. I soon learned I was no match for the fleet-footed Forest Service and had to content myself with staying at camp making life as uncomfortable as possible for 'The Rooster'.

Sitting outside the main tent, I heard the radio crackle into life and, uninvited, I stepped in to listen to the exchange about to take place.

The Rooster reported the protesters were still very much in evidence and things weren't going terribly well.

'Good,' I interjected, 'that's what I like to hear.'

The official on the receiving end began raving about the support the beleaguered shooters had from the chairman of the Park Board, and said that the police were being sent to the island, arriving some time that day. He further sought to bolster The Rooster's confidence by announcing: 'The Minister of Lands and the Minister of Forests both support you. You've got the backing of both of them.'

Rooster blushed to his hairline as I looked straight at him, grinning from ear to ear. 'Gosh, you guys really are on the ball,' I teased, for The Rooster knew, as I did, that the same man controlled the portfolios of Lands and Forests, but the official who worked for that Minister was ignorant of the fact.

'For Christ's sake, shut up!' shouted The Rooster and slammed the radio switch to 'Off'.

I tossed off a few flippantly appropriate comments and left the tent as Rob arrived hard on the heels of two disgruntled-looking foot soldiers. Although not privvy to the conversation, we could overhear enough to know the shooters were not happy with the situation and the interference of the protesters and had decided to call it quits for the day.

The Rooster, his feathers still ruffled from the radio communique, stalked over to where we sat and flicked open a blue, plastic folder containing a badge and his credentials.

'What's your name, boy?' he demanded of Rob.

Rob grinned at him and proceeded to wipe the perspiration from his face.

'I said, what's your name?'

I leaned back on my elbows, feeling full of mischief.

'Where did you get that badge, Herr Kapitain — in a cornflakes box?'

By now, The Rooster was having trouble controlling himself and I couldn't blame him; it was a new situation for us all and we were testing one another in a rather charged atmosphere.

'The cops will take care of you,' he warned me and turned his attention back to Rob. With great skill and calm, Rob fobbed off the verbal third degree and succeeded in remaining anonymous.

The windswept camp site was a busy place with shooters, scientists and protesters wandering in and out dodging, following and shadowing one another. A proper game of cat and mouse it was and it wore on all our nerves. Yet those opposing the shoot maintained a sort of 'high', fed by excitement, fatigue and commitment. The whole scene was bizarre and at times I couldn't believe it was really happening.

What did seem real was the possibility of arrest when the police arrived and I wondered how I'd cope with this. I could see myself handcuffed and struggling, being dragged to the helicopter and hauled away, for I had determined I would not go quietly. The greatest worry was the thought of the children turning on the evening news and seeing their mother behind bars!

Ken came wearily into camp and dropped to the ground beside me and I told him The Rooster had mentioned the possibility of arrest. Ken promised he would bake me a cake with a hacksaw in it and come to see me on visiting days, coaxing me to laugh as we painted the scenario.

'Can't you see the headlines, Bet? "Goat lady arrested!" '

'I will not go quietly,' I promised The Rooster. 'I'll kick, scream, bite, claw — you'll have to drag me into the helicopter!'

The Rooster said nothing, but looked as if he relished the thought of doing the dragging and we settled down to await the long arm of the law.

It reached us about 3.30 in the afternoon, by which time I had talked myself into hard labour and a diet of bread and water. When the little red helicopter dropped the men in blue from the sky, I extracted a solemn promise from Ken to get me a good lawyer and to tell the family I loved them, and then stepped forward to meet my destiny. The Rooster looked smug and very like a cocky bantam as he welcomed the police and pointed in our direction.

The two policemen looked towards us and I tried to appear proud and defiant, while leaning on Ken for support, then they swept past and proceeded to set up their tent. Other than a fatherly pep-talk from one of them, the police treated us with indifference for the duration of the protest and The Rooster informed me that he had no intention of allowing me to get myself arrested and thereby become a martyr!

As I did not aspire to martyrdom, I thanked The Rooster for

placing himself between me and the arms of the law, promised him I would continue to be as civilly disobedient as possible without donning the cloak of Joan of Arc, and left for home.

The following morning we looked down from the ridge to see the occupants of the camp scrambling aboard a boat and heading south. A hasty conference on our part concluded they were heading for Wellington Bay and planned to put us off the scent. It had been a stroke of luck that we arrived when we did.

While the younger ones hot-footed it across the ridge, Ken and I hobbled into camp, deserted except for The Rooster and the two policemen. Ken swaggerd to the tent and lifting his hand to his head in a salute, smilingly announced: 'Liaison Officer Crisp reporting. Just wanted to tell you guys you won't be having any problems with our jokers this morning, they've gone mustering in Wellington Bay." And doffing his hat, he turned to leave. With a mug of coffee poised at his lips, The Rooster received the news by spluttering the contents of the cup across the tent, accompanied by a volley of unprintable oaths, and we knew that Wellington Bay was where it was all happening. Ken did an Irish jig out of the tent and I congratulated him on a remarkable performance.

When the shooters and scientists hit the beaches in Wellington Bay, they were helped ashore by the protesters; the shock and disbelief on their faces was a joy to behold.

The protest was a mixture of heartbreak and hilarity and, with the nuisance factor as our only weapon, we savoured every small victory. We had decided to protest as passively as possible and by our presence keep the shooters gun-shy. At best, it could only be a delaying action and all around us the goats were slowly dying and we were quickly sinking into exhausted impotence. The only one who could stop the killing was the Minister and he had given his blessing to it, with both heads. It was a crazy game with crazy rules which we made up as we went along, day after weary day.

Celia, relieved of her kitchen duties by two of the volunteers, sat with me on the hill waiting for the mists to lift. We had taken shelter under a tree along with Ken, who had decided to catch up on some rest. He selected a rock, stretched out on the damp ground and promptly fell into a deep sleep. From his water bed, with a pillow of rock, came contented snores and we marvelled at his ability to sleep under such conditions.

From deep within the mists came a song and Celia grabbed my hand, whispering, 'Do you hear someone singing?'

I did indeed, and our songster drew closer.

'C'mon, move along, that's a good girl. Here we go, that's the way, c'mon my dearie does.'

Peering through the swirling fog, we caught a glimpse of Yvonne walking slowly behind a small group of goats, gently waving her arms and sweetly singing them to safety. We moved quietly down the hill to intercept her and she greeted us with a beaming 'Good morning' and moved her charges along.

My dear, sweet Yvonne; so much love, so much goodness. Celia and I could only squeeze each other's hands to acknowledge a sunlit moment that had lighted our path in the gloom.

For me, Yvonne's gentle efforts told the story of the protest; moving ourselves and the goats around like pawns on a chessboard, knowing that within the confines of the island, it was only a matter of time until the animals were found and the shooters cried 'Checkmate!' There was an unbearable reality about our inability to do anything except delay the inevitable.

Celia and I returned to find Mark Blackburn sitting with Ken. Mark was a close friend who had been with us for many a muster and had earned his stripes in the battle for the wildlife. He and Ken decided to head for the camp and see what, if anything, was happening. Celia and I sat huddled together for warmth, discussing the week's events, when suddenly a shot rang out so close that we both flattened ourselves to the ground, faces down.

Two more shots followed and I whispered into Celia's ear, 'My God, Celia, those shots came from the direction of Ken and Mark. I've got to see if they are all right.'

I crawled commando-style to the top of the knoll and listened intently for any sound. I almost jumped out of my skin when another shot rang out above me and watched horrified as a little buck vaulted head over heels past where I crouched, then lay dying with half its side blown away. I could make out two figures above me and a small group of goats below milling about in frightened confusion. I saw the shooter raise his rifle and something inside exploded. I jumped to my feet and, screaming like a wild animal, raced pell-mell down the steep incline towards the goats. I tripped and fell and screamed again as I landed heavily on a boulder. Staggering to my feet, I picked up rocks and hurled them at the goats below to make them run. I screamed until I was hoarse: 'Run, run. Don't just stand there, run!' With tails up and beards flying, they raced out of sight.

I sank to the ground and buried my head in my hands, sobbing.

When I looked up, the shooters were gone. I remembered Celia and climbed back to the place I'd left her, but found only her cap and the imprint of where our bodies had hugged the earth.

'Celia, Celia, where are you?' I cried, and heard her reply from below. I hugged her to me and we cried some more. She had heard the shot, then my screams and had assumed something terrible had happened. She was on her way to search for me when she heard my call. We calmed each other and sat warming ourselves as the sun peered through the mist.

'Celia, do you think your family will believe this when you write to them about it?'

'My mother will be horrified,' she said. And we laughed as we had cried, deeply and lustily. For two relatively quiet, peace-loving, middle-aged souls like us, it had been quite a week. We sat alone on the desolate hillside, eyes puffed and red-rimmed with crying, faces caked with mud, and talked of the quiet life we both had aspired to and which seemed an impossible dream, if the events of the morning were anything to go by.

Having regained our composure and laughed ourselves back into good humour, Celia decided that we should do what we had come to do — hassle the opposition. We moved on to the ridge overlooking the camp site and, by shedding our outer clothing and parkas, dressed three bushes to resemble people sitting on the hill. Then we crept closer to the camp and made goat-like noises, darting back to where our bush manikins waited. Men flew out of the tents, binoculars raised, watching as we stood and 'chatted' with our friends. When they had returned to the tents, we gathered our clothes, circled the camp and repeated the performance, giggling like schoolgirls at the commotion we caused. Slipping quietly through the bush, we stopped and screamed, then moved to another spot and gobbled like turkeys. Back and forth we went, roaring, trumpeting, neighing and, in a grand finale, we stood flapping our arms and gave a loud 'Cock-a-doodle-doo . . .' in honour of The Rooster. We had an absolutely grand time and hugged each other with each flurry of activity we created at the camp. It was crazy, zany, undignified (and unnerving for our tent dwellers below) and we enjoyed every moment of it.

On the way back up to the ridge, we met a group of seven protesters and told them of our escapades. Someone in the group decided there was still time enough left for one more round of mischief-making before we headed home and we came out on the knob above the camp. Our voices, deliberately raised, served to attract the attention of the camp's inmates and, as pre-arranged, we walked single file across the knob and disappeared into thick bush. Once lost from sight, we dashed madly to the end of the line, exchanging hats and jerseys to give us a different appearance. Our little group of nine, marching in circles, must have looked like an army advancing on the camp site, for we heard one voice exclaim: 'There must be hundreds of them!' and we dissolved into laughter. Dad's Army of nine marched around the walls of Jericho and tricked the opposing forces into believing we were a legion!

Mitch observed the weariness in his ageing mother as he helped me down the hill that night and I confided to him that I was rapidly losing my ability to climb every mountain, day after day. Even the younger protestors were showing signs of wear and tear and the 'oldies' were definitely feeling their age.

Mitch suggested we make our headquarters on the ridge overlooking the Forest Service camp, thereby eliminating half our daily footwork. Everyone agreed this was an excellent idea. Fortunately, some of the volunteers had come equipped with tents and canvases to stretch between bushes. The following morning we hauled, not only ourselves to the ridge top but also shelter, enough food and water to last for several days, and some thirst-quenching home-brew.

Oh, the joy of bidding The Rooster goodnight and unpleasant dreams, then climbing to the ridge, knowing we would have to go no further! That night we slept under the stars and a full yellow moon. Ashley delighted us all with a quickly conceived explanation for our presence on the mountain top.

'Okay, everybody,' Ashley shouted from his tent, just moments after we had settled for the night. 'This is Rowe's Safari Tours.'

'Oh, Ashley, go to sleep,' laughed Yvonne.

Strutting around the camp, he continued: 'For a modest fee, you can partake of all the wonders of Arapawa Island. Chip in a little extra and you can spend the day chasing goats and shooters!'

Someone threw a boot at him and others crawled out of their tents to watch. He knelt beside Mitch and Mark Blackburn, who were stretched out on the ground under a sagging piece of canvas.

'And the nights, oh la la, you spend them in sumptuous, elegant accommodation.'

Mitch groaned and yelled for Yvonne to come and get him, but Ashley danced to the centre of the camp.

'Morning tea is served, courtesy of the Forest Service and then,

Mama mia, the best is yet to come! For no extra charge you can assist in a scientific breakthrough. You can discover if the wild sheep object to grazing in the middle of a firing range!'

By now everyone was up and merrily chasing Ashley around, threatening him with every conceivable punishment if he didn't go back to his tent and let us get some sleep.

He dodged us nimbly, crying, 'Wait, wait, there is more. I have arranged for you all to have an autographed picture of The Rooster!'

If there had been water to spare, I think Ashley, with his friendly tour guide pitch, would have been dowsed then and there.

Mark cracked the tops from two bottles of brew and with paper cups half full we wandered to the edge and sat looking out over the channel. Below us we could hear the goats and Yvonne wondered aloud what the morrow would hold for them.

'They'll probably be dead,' said Ken softly and with bitterness. Ken's remark opened the door for the, as yet, unspoken feelings of some of the younger protesters. They felt that we should take more desperate action, although none suggested any physical violence. There was a division of opinion as to how we should conduct ourselves, and the older ones among us cautioned against anything other than passive resistance. In retrospect, I believe we should have done something more dramatic, such as throwing the ammunition into the sea or diverting their water supply, but no matter what we did, we could only postpone the inevitable. The spell was broken and we made our way dejectedly back to our beds.

The next morning Sid arrived with an urgent message from Arthur asking me to meet him in Wellington. The Minister of Lands had indicated that he would see Arthur and me to discuss the situation on the island, and Arthur felt it might be our last chance to stop the shooting. Arthur, secretary of the Trust, had travelled far and wide on behalf of the Arapawa wildlife, composed numerous submissions and had established a home for a small number of the animals at Spencer Park, where he was the manager. Like so many who came before and after, Arthur had contributed enormously to the ongoing battle for the wildlife and I believe he considers the conversation issues on Arapawa to be among the most difficult he has fought for. While we were playing cat and mouse with the Forest Service, Arthur had kept the protest alive in the media and had been pressing vigorously for an audience with the Minister; it seemed that he had succeeded.

For my part, Wellington was a hundred light years away and thoughts of the effort it would take to get there numbed me.

'I just can't do it!' I wailed as Celia packed my clothes. 'Celia, I'm just *too* tired." But Celia rang for a water-taxi. I slept all the way to the capital, moving in a dream as I was deposited by friends on to the various forms of transport that got me there. Shelia Ramsay met me at the airport and took me to the People's Palace where I remained comatose until dinner the next day.

Arthur flew from Christchurch and together we received the news that the Minister would not see us after all! We marched indignantly to Broadcasting House and gave them a story that in no uncertain terms told of our displeasure.

Shelia and I stayed on for two days after Arthur left and invaded Parliament, stomping the halls and speaking to anyone we could manoeuvre into a corner. Many of the then Labour opposition tried to assist us, and I remember Fraser Colman spending 45 minutes trying to contact the Minister of Lands and Forests on our behalf. David Lange introduced us to his research staff and Mary Batchelor received us with warmth and understanding.

Upon my return to Aotea, the last of the protesters boarded the water-taxi as I alighted from it, affording me only a glimpse of those who had arrived in my absence. The protest was over and everyone, including the Forest Service, was going home. I noted with alarm the dark purple circles around the eyes of those who remained and wondered if they would ever recover from the strain. I felt like Methuselah.

The Forest Service claimed they had killed 2,000 goats and dumped them into 'an inaccessible gully' somewhere on the island. Two thousand decaying animals would have made their presence known far from the island and, although we searched, we could never find this gully which I believe was so inaccessible that it never existed.

The numbers shot have always been disputed. We were there and saw what was happening. On one occasion the Forest Service claimed a daily kill of 300 plus, but there had been only ten shots fired, which would have made them extraordinarily skilled marksmen! When confronted, they hastily printed a retraction, but the numbers of goats killed mounted into the thousands in order to justify their actions. Perhaps the most unbelievable directive from the Minister of Lands and Forests came when he ordered the capture of 100 Arapawa goats while the shooting was still in progress! Despite the ignorance of The Rooster's radio colleague, the Minister of Lands and the Minister of Forests were one and the same, but he obviously didn't talk to himself. Having sent the foot soldiers to the front to exterminate the goats, he now sent in the airborne forces to rescue 100 of them to 'preserve the gene pool'!

Having labelled them 'scrubbers, valueless, part-Angora and a mixed-bag', he was now spending taxpayers' money to preserve what he was also spending taxpayers' money to exterminate.

The Minister was hedging his bets, just in case we were right all along; then he could say he had made contingency plans to save the breed. Did he think the double standard and double expense would appease both parties? We were not appeased and could not allow this muddle that passed for Ministerial wisdom to go unchallenged. The physical part of the protest was over and we could but weep for the dead and promise those that survived that we would never give up.

CHAPTER XII

All In April

Mary announced she was going to be married and Roy wore a hound-dog expression each time he came home, perking up only when it was time to depart and return to the arms of his beloved.

It takes perception on the part of a parent to differentiate between teenage daydreaming and true introspective thought; between the genuine search for identity and the glazed gazings of a youth whose hormones keep throwing him into extremes of emotion.

I had not perceived the signs of maturity and had cocooned myself into believing we were five against the world, despite signals from the children to the contrary. That we would ever be anything other than a quintet had not penetrated my conscious thinking, for I saw us as unit of survival in a hostile and polluted world, far from the maddening crowd and the Doomsday clock that read five to midnight.

While Walt and I had been dodging flying foxes, coping with Old Man Southerly and arguing with Knowledgables, the children had synchronised the adolescent tangle of arms and legs, fitting them nicely into lithe and mature bodies, had smoothed creaking vocal chords and come to the realisation that musical appreciation did not necessarily mean the radio volume had to break the sound barrier. Furry chins had become luxuriant beards covering that sometimes rebellious jut of the chin and a well-groomed look had overtaken both their personal appearances and their bedrooms, a telltale sign in itself.

I woke one morning to find myself redundant — my services as chief guide and counsellor were no longer needed. Somehow my dimpled darlings of yesterday had skipped from childhood dependence to adolescence to maturity before I'd noticed. And now they stood before me, or more precisely towered above me, declaring their independence of the parent-child relationship, while in the next breath committing themselves totally to a new relationship and an ever greater dependency.

Mary had found her Adonis, a golden Kiwi, broad-shouldered, personable and with a heart-stopping grin. We congratulated her on her excellent taste, eyed the bank balance uneasily and found ourselves humming 'Here comes the bride'. Mary moved through her pre-wedding days in a state of high tension and excitement befitting any bride-to-be, while Roy continued to be starry-eyed and vaguely discontented unless he was expounding the virtues of a certain young woman we had yet to meet.

Mitch viewed all this love-struck behaviour through the eyes of a dedicated bachelor, humbugging it all with the grace of Scrooge, and pitying his younger siblings for falling into the tender trap. Never, he informed anyone who would listen, would such a fate befall him.

Mary's looks in Walt's direction when he suggested she and Mark elope and that he would pay for the ladder and the getaway boat, told us she did not appreciate her father's attempt at humour. She wanted a full-dress regalia, complete with 'something borrowed, old, new and blue'. Walt responded by indicating the borrowed bit would be the loan we would have to take at 10% interest to pay for the wedding and blue, he cracked, would be our reaction to a very red bank balance! Although our chosen way of life offered many rewards, none of them had anything to do with accumulation of wealth, and Mary and her Adonis were destined to pay for a good share of their own wedding.

Our second thought, after the elopement suggestion failed, was to have the wedding at Aotea but, given the unpredictable weather, it was decided a safer course of action was to tie the knot in Blenheim.

Preparing for a wedding under normal conditions is, by all accounts, nerve-wracking and our position on the island could hardly be deemed 'normal'. Back and forth we sailed to the mainland attending showers, buying gifts, selecting suitable clothing for the occasion and always stopping first at the bank. We had a meeting with Mark's parents, more bank consultation, fittings, and sessions with the caterers. All in all, we covered the waterway from Arapawa to the mainland more times in the month preceding the wedding than we had in the previous two years.

Walt's brother and sister-in-law arrived from the States for the occasion and what a grand reunion it was. We talked long into the nights and pored over the family photographs they had brought, trying to guess who was who among the nieces and nephews, many of whom had grown to maturity since we had last seen them.

Aotea was a totally new experience for John and Margie but they settled into our rustic comforts with remarkable ease. The only difficulty arose when they left the circle of light bestowed by the four kerosene lanterns hanging from the cartwheel and groped in vain for a light switch on the wall of the bathroom or bedroom. John found himself forever stumbling about in the dark until he eventually remembered to pluck a lantern from the wheel and take it with him.

Prior to their arrival, it had rained almost continuously for a week and we were becoming increasingly concerned about Ashley and Yvonne around in East Bay. They had not yet built their cabin and were living in a small tent the width of a double mattress. It could be that Yvonne and Ashley's mattress, lying as it was between them and the sodden earth, was rapidly becoming a waterbed. Mitch went to check on their situation and offered to bring them back to Aotea, an invitation they happily accepted. Not only had their bed turned into one of cold, damp comfort, but their clothing had taken on a distinctly musty aroma, accompanied by spots of mildew.

The weather situation had made washing clothes a waste of time and energy, leaving us with very little to choose from as we sought to find them a change of clothing. Much rummaging around produced an oversize shirt and baggy trousers for Yvonne and Ashley was handed a piece of gaudy material which Mitch had brought home from his adventures in the South Seas. Ashley wrapped this around his waist, topped it with an old plaid skirt, his bare feet protruding below.

They were attired in this fashion when Margie and John arrived and, after the initial hugs and kisses, I turned to introduce them to Ashley in flowing lava-lava and Yvonne in menswear, her hair tucked up under a cap. Margie's face was a study as she tried to decipher which name fitted the appropriately clad gender. Ashley stood, wiggling his toes and, without speaking, beamed a big welcoming smile. Margie took me to one side and asked discreetly: 'Does she, er . . . ah . . . he speak English?'

It dawned on me that to the eyes of the uninitiated, Ashley, brown eyes dancing, barefooted and wrapped in a sarong, probably looked like the pictures of a smiling islander Margie had seen on a travel brochure, especially since all she had received from him was a beaming, white-toothed grin. We had to disappoint her by declaring Ashley to be simply a slightly sodden pakeha who spoke a somewhat different version of the common language.

Communications were established, although John and Margie's Yankee accent was not always understood and Ashley and Yvonne's colloquialisms at times brought conversation to a standstill. Overall it was a happy, if somewhat faltering, exchange and it gave Margie and John an opportunity to meet and enjoy two very fine New Zealanders.

Since our English friends Celia and Sid had left us to take up a position across the sound in Endeavour Inlet, Yvonne and Ashley agreed to look after the farm and animals for the few days we would be in town for the wedding. The April showers cleared enough on the day before to allow us a dry, although not altogether comfortable, trip to the mainland. We arrived at a house full of excitement and anticipation on par with the frenzy of someone who has left all their shopping until nine o'clock on a Christmas Eve. Dozens of last-minute details needed attention, the phone rang urgently from Mary's to Mark's and back again, and Mary had a king-sized case of pre-nuptial nerves that spread to the rest of us. From the sound of things, the wedding would have to be postponed at least a week; it didn't seem possible things could fall into place in a mere 24 hours.

A fitful night's sleep, then a morning with more crises and more phone calls. The petticoat for one of the bridesmaids could not be found and the flowers had not been delivered. When they finally were tracked down and brought to the flat, the carnations for the men were missing. Mark was in a state of shock and it appeared that all the months of planning and preparation had been for nothing.

The only ones who remained untouched by the chaos were John and Margie, who laughed until they cried as the countdown continued and the tension mounted. Having been through the trauma of their own daughter's wedding, they could sit back and enjoy all the pre-wedding tumult.

Walt, his usually calm approach to life slightly frayed at the edges, sat by the phone relaying urgent messages from the home of the groom and passing on anxious instructions from Mary. He had no sooner replaced the receiver after reassuring the bridesmaid her petticoat had been found alive and well, when the phone rang yet again. Margie rolled with laughter as Walt reached for the receiver and greeted the caller: 'This is the cool, calm, collected father of the bride; what can I do for you?'

'Well!' said a frazzled Mrs Jackson. 'I'm glad things are calm and collected at your end, because they are certainly in a mess here!'

Fate had delivered a final coup d'etat at the eleventh hour. If we thought we had problems, it was nothing compared to what the Jacksons were going through. Mark's sister, travelling from the West Coast and still many kilometres from Blenheim, had just rung to say that her car had broken down, whereupon Mark's father had jumped into his car and dashed to the rescue. Given the distance he had to go, it seemed unlikely they would get back in time for the wedding.

Poor Mrs Jackson sounded almost in tears and Walt did his best to console her.

As I helped Mary to dress and made my own final preparations, I could feel the lump starting to rise in my throat and noticed Walt looked a bit dewy-eyed as Mary stepped into the lounge and everyone oohed and aahed approvingly. The cars lined up to drive Mary and her entourage to the church and as we watched, Mary, a vision in white, swept from the house followed by the bridesmaids and assorted guests. The wedding party filled the first few cars while the other guests occupied the remaining seats in the cavalcade.

I began to feel a bit uneasy as one by one the cars drove off in a flurry of streamers and laughter, the occupants waving cheerily and calling 'See you in church' and we waited for one of the cars to stop for us. My uneasiness turned to disbelief as the last of the cars pulled away and disappeared around the corner, leaving John, Margie, Walt and I resplendent in our wedding refinery and quite devoid of transport!

We learned later that each of the drivers had assumed we had our own car and were seeing the wedding party off before sedately bringing up in the rear. I hadn't the foggiest notion where the church was and could only give the taxi driver, whom we had rung in a state of panic, the name of the vicar who was to perform the service. The driver looked at us somewhat askance when we explained we were the parents, uncle and aunt of the bride whom we had inadvertently lost.

'Darling!'

'Yes, dear?' answered Walt, unaccustomed to such endearments.

'Not you,' I snapped. 'Darling, that's the name of the vicar!'

'Right you are, lady,' said our obliging taxi driver. 'I'm R.C. myself, but I think I know where this Darling fellow works.'

I sat behind the driver urging him on as we were already several minutes behind the wedding party and things couldn't proceed without us. We careened around a corner and pulled up beside a deserted church.

Where was everybody? The guests, the family, the groom — and where was Mary?

'Oh Lord,' I moaned, 'this must be the wrong church!'

'Well, lady, this is Darling's place. I'm sure of it.'

'Maybe I got the wrong vicar. Walt, what shall we do?' I was feeling on the verge of hysteria by now. Margie hadn't stopped laughing since we found ourselves stranded, and out tumbled a fresh volley of hilarity as Walt rushed into the church to see if we had the right place and I dashed, blue skirts held high, to the phone box to ring Mrs Jackson.

The driver drummed his fingers nervously on the wheel, casting sideways glances that left little doubt as to his appraisal of this zany quartet, two of whom claimed they had a daughter they couldn't find, about to be married in a church of unknown address by a man of the cloth whose name they weren't sure of. One woman seemed beset by hysterical laughter while the other teetered precariously between hand-wringing frustration as she beseeched the Lord to lead her to her daughter's wedding and moments of high-pitched giggles that ended in hiccups. The men appeared dazed, and to top it off they all spoke with American accents.

The poor man's consternation no doubt deepened when Walt returned with the news that he had found our 'Darling' and indeed the wedding was to take place in about an hour.

I slid into the back seat after having had a rather animated phone discussion with Mrs Jackson as I added to her dilemma by explaining we had lost the wedding party and did she have any idea where they could be? She replied with the information that the bride and company had gone for pre-wedding photographs and we, as the parents of the bride, were expected to be present.

'There's just one little problem,' I smiled weakly at the driver.

He raised his eyebrows and sucked in his chin in anticipation.

'We, ah, that is, Mrs Jackson, isn't quite sure just where the photographer is.'

The driver put his fingers to his temples and shrugged his shoulders. 'Okay, lady, can you at least give me a clue?'

I relayed what little information Molly had given me and off we roared up one street and down another until we turned a corner and, with great relief, saw the cars with streamers flying and guests milling about.

'Where were you?' reproached Mary as we ran breathlessly in the door.

'It's a long story, honey. I'll tell you later.'

Molly Jackson and I walked slowly to the front of the church together since Mr Jackson had not yet returned from his rescue mission. As we made our way down the aisle, nodding and smiling, Molly muttered through clenched teeth: 'I have *never* had such a day in my entire life!'

I whispered my whole-hearted agreement as we parted company and slid into our seats on either side of the aisle.

Mary looked radiant and Walt so proud as he guided her down the church. Mitch and Roy supported Mark and seeing them standing there together, so young and full of life, filled me with love and pride.

A flurry of activity in the side aisle caught my attention. Hurrying down to the front pew was Mr Jackson, knotting his tie as he slid in beside his wife just in time to hear 'Dearly beloved . . .'

Mark beamed and grinned his big warm smile as Walt placed Mary's hand in his and, in response to the call, 'Who giveth this woman to be married?' replied in a clear, strong voice, 'Her mother and I.'

My eyes were already swimming and I felt a catch in my throat. All it took was the pat on the back from Margie who leaned forward in sympathy and the floodgates opened. The more I tried not to cry, the more certain it became that the tears would flow and I sniffed and dabbed through the rest of the service.

The day after the wedding we sailed for home to be greeted by the heavily laden skies and sheets of rain that had bid us bon voyage three days before. According to Ashley, the rain had continued in our absence and the predictions were for more of the same. Yvonne had managed to dry a few of their clothes by hanging some in the greenhouse and others on a shelf above Little Bertha. John and Margie were due to leave at the end of the week and were anxious to start the last lap of their journey with clean clothing. Clean we could get the clothes, dry we could not.

To compound the problem, I received a letter from Arthur informing me he had arranged a meeting with the Minister and would I join him, Ken and Bruce Candy in Wellington, via the next mailboat?

Now I too had to join the already overcrowded laundry queue and within two days, try to rustle up enough clean, dry clothing for a week's travelling and suitable for meeting with a Knowledgable. A coat of protective armour to stave off the slings and arrows of outrageous bureaucracy would have served me best, but all I had to choose from were my second-hand misfits and the mother-of-the-bride finery. Somehow I couldn't picture myself sweeping into the Minister's office arrayed in heavenly blue and plunging neckline to plead the case for the goats, nor did gumboots and baggy breeches seem appropriate. I therefore rang Celia with the news that we were off to see the Wizard, that wonderful wizard of Long Gully, and could she lend me something for the occasion. As always, Celia came to the rescue and I prepared to leave.

Margie and John graciously understood that I must leave them before their time of departure and, while they did not fully understand the depth of my commitment, they somehow sensed the urgency and, as did so many of those I loved, they assumed second place to the Arapawa wildlife. It seemed that my concern for the animals would intrude forever into my life and the lives of those around me but, because I knew I could not leave their fate to the Knowledgables, I swallowed my feelings of guilt and embarrassment and began packing.

Just before I was due to leave, friends called in and, when they learned of Yvonne and Ashley's desire to return to East Bay, they kindly volunteered transport. Our friends' boat was not a large one and it was suggested that plastic bags containing the neatly wrapped, hard-won dry clothing be placed in the dinghy behind. With a farewell and a roar, they left the jetty, creating a wake of considerable proportions and sending up a spray that fell into the dinghy saturating all we had laboured so long to dry. Yvonne and Ashley returned to their little tent as sodden as when they had left.

I departed next, with a tearful farewell, and headed for Wellington. Arthur and I had covered this same territory many times in the past and were to do so many times in the future. Ken and I had hassled and harangued through the protest and sweated through the musters. Bruce and I had written submission after submission on behalf of the wildlife and, during the third muster, Bruce had carried one of the bucks from the axial ridge to the beach and returned to help me as I struggled with a particularly uncooperative billy. Many others carried animals that day, but Bruce had done so with a dislocated shoulder. He had had a fall the week before the scheduled third rescue attempt and arrived black, blue and strapped. It had been obvious Bruce was in pain, but he never asked to be excused from the rigours of the muster.

The four old warriors of the Arapawa saga tried yet again to penetrate the impenetrable, with the same lack of success that characterised all such meetings with Knowledgables. Possessed of an inertia, lumbered with a pragmatism that disallows inventive thought, the Knowledgables stayed true to form and could think of nothing better than bending inept policies. The only positive thing that came out of the trip to Wellington was an extensive amount of television coverage for our cause. We were not aware that the news media knew about our meeting or, in fact, still considered us newsworthy, and it was with surprise and amusement that we watched the television crew sweep past the Minister and his fawning entourage and rush towards us! It was all the more amusing since the upstaging took place in the Minister's own outer office and it must have been particularly annoying to him to know that the subject matter which claimed the media's attention was a herd of goats!

We happily gave the reporters the story and my own feelings of frustration were not spared in the telling. Over the years, the media has treated us kindly and I have appreciated their attention and response. Without them, the struggle for survival of the Arapawa wildlife would have remained known only to a few.

The next day Arthur, Ken and Bruce sat with me at Wellington airport awaiting my flight home. For some reason, now forgotten, I had decided to fly instead of taking the ferry. Walt had farewelled his brother and sister-in-law and would meet me at the airport in Blenheim.

Our meeting the day before had included a very heated exchange with the chairman of the Park Board who had been summoned to Wellington for the occasion, and Arthur nudged me as that official walked into the terminal. I surmised he would be heading for Blenheim and had no doubt that we were scheduled for the same flight.

Our relationship was hardly cordial and there had been many intense disagreements over the years concerning the Arapawa wildlife. He and his board held the fate of the animals in their hands and, with the exception of one or two members who sincerely tried to assist us, the board remained lacking in sympathy or understanding.

It was difficult to determine whether the chairman saw us in the crowd or whether our meeting was a chance encounter that he would have preferred to avoid. Whatever the circumstances, our paths crossed and we exchanged a few strained words. Only the day before, we had locked swords across a conference table. During that exchange, I had risen from my chair as if jet-propelled and, as my feet touched the floor, my fist had hit the table in an angry retaliation to this man's accusations. Ken later described me as resembling a little terrier taking on a bulldog.

As we struggled to make small talk to hide the awkwardness we felt, Ken asked the chairman if he was flying to Blenheim. As he said 'Yes' and drew his ticket from his pocket, I was able to see his seat number and realised that we would be opposite ends of the plane. While Arthur and the others were heaving a sigh of relief at this seating arrangement, I excused myself from the group and, after enquiring at the ticket counter, was able to secure a seat next to the chairman.

Arthur was horrified when he heard what I had done for, although the trip was a short one, the chairman and I needed very little time to get under one another's skin and Arthur had visions of a very disrupted flight. He insisted I ring him later in the day to let him know what had happened. I assured my three friends that my intentions were honourable though I teased Arthur that he would probably read all about it in the evening paper. 'Hijacking over Cook Strait' it would read. 'Woman hijacks plane and instructs the pilot to fly to Timbuktu, deposit another passenger and leave him there, all the while shouting something about liberation for goats'.

I left Ken, Bruce and Arthur collectively shaking their heads as I walked to the plane beside the chairman and we took our seats. What I really had in mind was an opportunity to try to talk quietly and civilly without the rancour that had accompanied every previous meeting. That short trip to Blenheim was one of the few times the chairman and I have spoken on reasonable terms. When we left the plane I offered my hand and suggested we let bygones be bygones. My hand was accepted, but not the olive branch.

Walt watched this performance from the waiting room with mouth agape, for he knew that very little of a pacific nature had ever passed between the chairman and me and the closest we'd come to touch therapy had been when our chins met in stubborn resistance over numerous conference tables.

'What in the name of sense was that all about?' asked Walt in complete amazement.

'I offered the hand of friendship.'

'Was it accepted?'

'Only time will tell.'

In the ebb and flow of life some things change while others remain static. The chairman and I remained diametrically opposed and the handshake became meaningless. Eleven years of conflict have not changed attitudes towards the wildlife issues.

What was changing, however, was the composition of the family. Mary and Mark were about to make their duet a trio, and Roy was bringing the love of his life to meet us at long last.

Mary sat opposite me, looking contentedly pregnant, knitting small things, and I mentioned that Roy was finally about to let us have a look at the mysterious Marcia.

'I've met her, Mom, and she's really nice — you'll like her.'

I felt reassured by Mary's assessment and as we chatted, I pressed for details about the girl who had my baby's head in such a spin.

'There's just one thing you should know, Mom.'

'What's that, honey?'

Mary was knitting furiously now. 'Ah, er, well, she has a little son.'

'A son!'

Mary studied her pattern intently.

'Is she bringing him with her?' I asked, somewhat stunned by the revelation.

'No,' Mary replied slowly, 'she's bringing her daughter.'

'Daughter?' I gasped.

Mary kept her attention on her knitting, darting quick encouraging smiles in my direction as she tried to gauge my reaction.

I returned her smiles weakly, contemplating Mary's gently rounded stomach.

'How old are the children?' I asked, regaining my equilibrium and trying to sound calm and collected.

'I think Rickie is 5 and Loren is 1.'

'So,' I looked straight at Mary, 'she's bringing Loren?'

Mary made no reply and I felt a bit unnerved by it all.

'Is she a well-behaved one-year-old?' I ventured, sensing Mary was keeping some terrible truth from me.

'Well, actually Mom, she's a well-behaved three-year-old.'

'I thought you said she was one!'

Mary took a deep breath. 'Loren is one. Rachael is three.'

'My God, Mary, how many are there?'

Obviously relieved that things were out in the open, Mary continued, 'Marc has three children, Mom.'

'Three!' I whispered.

Mary nodded her head.

'Is Roy very serious?' I asked, trying to absorb the implications and remain in control.

'Very,' answered Mary firmly.

'Well,' I stammered, 'we'll have to break this to your father gently. We'll wait until he's all relaxed and in a very good mood and tell him about the children one by one. Yes, we'll most definitely have to break this gently.'

'Break what gently?' came Walt's suspicious query from the kitchen where he had entered unnoticed.

'Roy's girl-friend has three children!' I blurted out, holding up the appropriate number of fingers for emphasis.

'That's not exactly gentle, Mom.'

Walt lowered himself into the nearest chair.

'Well, Grandad,' I teased weakly, 'nothing like becoming instant grandparents.'

'Three grandchildren!' said Walt in disbelief.

'Four,' Mary reminded him, patting her tummy.

After the initial shock, I had to admit, I really wasn't surprised that Roy had chosen a ready-made family. He was a family sort of person and would make a good father. His own background of being an adopted child would enable him to be sensitive to the children's feelings and their acceptance of him as their stepfather.

Mitch mumbled something incoherent when told he was probably going to become Uncle Mitch to a lot of little people all at once and said he'd reserve his judgment until he'd met Marcia and had a good talk with her as to her intentions regarding his little brother!

I wondered what her thoughts about us must be. After hearing me on the radio and seeing me on television jumping up and down about the goats, she probably thought she was being brought to meet the Dragonlady, and I must have appeared a very formidable potential mother-in-law. This reputation of mine was, I had surmised, why Roy had taken so long to bring her to Aotea. Now, I realised Marcia's numerous offspring might have had something to do with the delay.

Mother-in-law, Grandmother! Everything seemed to be happening very fast indeed.

I watched Marcia come up the path to the house holding three-year-old Rachael by the hand and I liked what I saw.

'Poor kid,' I thought. 'She's probably terrified of what our reaction will be.'

Tall and willowy, Marcia gave the illusion of fragility which I soon discovered was far from the case. Both internally and externally, she possesses a strength and reserve of energy that has made those of rounder proportions and sturdier limbs blanch as they tried to keep up with her.

She had managed to keep her family of three together over the years and had sworn off the opposite sex forever until one day she looked out of her window and across the fence of the adjoining yard and met Roy's gaze.

Actually, Roy's attention had been drawn to the window by some rather shrill commands and unladylike language as Marc endeavoured to discipline her three uncooperative offspring. Having put them all to bed, she had moved to close the window and looked down into the amused, friendly eyes of my youngest.

'Hi!' she had said in a somewhat embarrassed voice, realising that her outburst had been overheard.

Roy was recovering from a heartache of his own and had no intention of becoming involved again, so they turned to one another in platonic friendship. They watched television, played games with the children and Roy became the babysitter so Marc could have the occasional night out. Thus it had all begun.

Now, this tall confident woman stood before me holding the hand of a pretty little blond-headed child who threw me completely off balance by calling me 'Nana' five minutes after they arrived!

Roy nudged me and gave me an impish grin. 'Hey, Mom, that's you Rachael is talking to. You!'

I mumbled something in a flustered voice about being called 'Auntie Betty' until we got to know one another better, but Roy made it quite clear there was no need for any other name and, since I would soon be the little stranger's grandmother, I might as well get used to being called 'Nana'. However, I had difficulty in remembering to respond to the unaccustomed name and had to be reminded so many times that Rachael was speaking to me, the poor child must have thought the grandmother she was about to acquire was stone deaf.

Walt's instant response to 'Grandad' was no better than mine to 'Nana' and until we adjusted to the unfamiliar names which placed us squarely in the senior citizen bracket, we must have appeared not only deaf but dim-witted as well.

Samantha decided to bless the occasion of our first visit from Marc and Rachael by going into labour and, as with all else she attempted, she did it with flare and aplomb. I was so pleased when Marc said she and Rachael would like to stay with me as I sat by Sam. Actress supreme, Sam lay heaving and straining, a look of suffering and resignation on her face. I knelt beside her crooning words of sympathy and encouragement while Marc and Rachael witnessed their first caprine birthing. Sam gave a performance worthy of an Oscar and when she had wrung every ounce of pity, bread and assorted titbits from us, she calmly rose to her feet and walked over to where Rachael sat quietly munching a bright red apple. Neither the pangs of labour nor imminent motherhood could lessen Sam's interest in food and, without so much as a please or thank you, she took the apple from Rachael's hand and devoured it, whereupon she returned to her birthing with renewed vigour. She grunted and groaned, then rose as she passed a small amount of the water sac which emerged in the shape of a small red balloon and Rachael's eyes grew wide with wonder. Minutes before she had seen Samantha take in her bright red apple from one end and now this very similar looking object was emerging from her other end.

'Mummy,' she whispered, awed by the miracle she was witnessing, 'is that the apple?'

Marc and I rolled with laughter, delighting in the uncomplicated thinking of a three-year-old — what goes in must come out.

Sam showed signs of pique at our mirth at such a delicate time and once again captured our attention by throwing her head back and piercing the air with a primeval scream, pushing first one, then another Arapawa kid into the waiting cradle of straw. She rested only a moment, then with quick, flicking tongue, accompanied by a steady stream of guttural endearments, cleaned the babies from head to tail. She removed the mucus from their noses and mouths, nibbling the severed umbilical cord to within half an inch of their soft tawny coloured bellies. We watched enchanted as the little ones struggled to their feet, fighting off Sam's persistent attentions, searching for the milk-gorged teats.

I brought Sam some hay and warm water, then left her basking proudly in new-found maternal bliss. As Marc and I walked back to the house with Rachael between us, I felt a bond had been forged. Sam had worked her special caprine magic. Marc and I smiled at each other over Rachael's head and I knew Marc and her numerous offspring were going to be a welcome addition to the family.

The initial contact made, Roy soon found an opportunity to bring the entire family to Aotea for a camping trip and, before the week was out, Walt and I had grown accustomed to this sudden new dimension in our lives, responding without prompting to the 'Nana's and 'Grandad's issuing forth from Rickie, 5; Rachael, 3 and Loren, 1.

The following April, Roy and Marc were married with all the children in attendance along with Mary's new son, Mark Linsay, Jr, barely five weeks of age.

Mitch's protestations against love and marriage seemed to become distinctly less frequent and convincing after the arrival of a certain young lady to Aotea. We began to suspect that one of Cupid's arrows had penetrated his tough bachelor's hide, even though he vehemently denied any weakening of resolve.

Debbie had come to us after a grievous personal tragedy and it was in the presence of this beautiful, tawny Fijian woman that Mitch's resolve began to melt away. As the romance developed, Mitch was reminded of his oft-spoken words about the joys of bachelorhood and, because he was fighting a losing battle, he was man enough to admit that Roy and Marc had been right after all: love was 'a many splendoured thing'.

While Roy and Marc had progressed towards their wedding slowly and deliberately, working through the pros and cons of Roy taking on a ready-made family and Marc taking on the Goat-lady for a mother-in-law, Mitch and Debbie, although late starters, passed quickly through the preliminary stages, caught up with Roy and Marc, and announced they would be married only weeks after Marcia became Mrs Rowe. Needless to say, that was a very busy April, but I remained convinced that marrying two sons in one month is infinitely easier than marrying one daughter.

In what seemed a whirlwind of hearts, flowers, orange blossom and wedding bells, we now had a large collection of in-laws and grandchildren. Family gatherings began to take on that wonderfully boisterous confusion I remembered so well from the times when Walt's brothers and sisters had come together in a gathering of the clan. I began to understand more fully the sustaining power of the family and why those moments of shared joy, love, grief, birthdays, christenings and Christmas had always been so important, and we strove to make them meaningful for our children's children. We had come full circle in the land of our choosing.

CHAPTER XIII

The 500 Metre Revolt

Leaving Aotea was like saying goodbye to a beloved child and it was several years before I could enter the homestead again without heartache. Aotea had been the Camelot of my dreams; the place where I'd make it all happen, where work and enthusiasm had known no bounds, where I'd talked to the animals, the trees, the birds, the bees and the breeze, and had been spoken to by voices across the abyss of time; where we'd screamed defiance at Old Man Southerly as he beat us into submission, subduing our arrogant assumptions of taming Mother Nature; where we'd cradled the green growing children of the garden, protecting them from ripping winds and rampaging bovines; where we'd dodged flying foxes and Forest Service bullets and cheered each other on with every successful step towards self-sufficiency. So many hopes, so many memories.

New Zealand was to have been the land of happy-ever-after, where we would live unpolluted lives beside pristine streams and let the rest of the world go by. We would blaze an organic trail of self-sufficiency and walk gently upon the earth, leaving neither footprint nor scar. How bursting with ideals and ideas we had been and how naive to believe we could make them come true.

I lived alone now with these memories. We had crammed several lifetimes and such vast experience into one brief shining hour, that I could spend many hours in reverie and not recall everything that had happened. My involvement with the Arapawa wildlife had opened new avenues of thought for me, avenues I had not yet fully explored and I discovered that many of these thoughts were having a disquieting effect upon my acceptance of things never questioned before.

I had come in contact with many caring people as a result of the fight for the wildlife and, as a result, I had become aware of the animal liberation movement. Without realising it, I had started my own little animal liberation revolution on the island and it was a natural progression that my feelings, inclined as they were towards the rights of the animals, should be strongly affected by what I learned from those who were already deeply committed and involved.

At first I ignored the still, small voice within that whispered 'hypocrite' as I thumped the pulpit righteously on behalf of the goats while happily sitting down to a home-grown roast mutton dinner, and refused to draw a parallel between the tragedy of the wildlife and my own contribution to the sufferings of the sheep upon whom our existence depended.

At the same time as I was involved in my soul-searching activities, Walt and I were entering upon a middle-age crisis. It all boiled over in a finale of Shakespearean proportions and I flung myself from the hallowed halls of Aotea, taking my principles, my three dogs, a vegetarian cookbook and my goats with me. I didn't go far, only to a bach at the head of the bay some 500 metres from the homestead.

But I could well have crossed an ocean, so great had the gulf grown between Walt and myself. It had taken me some time to face the fact that all was not well, and to admit that for me, at least, the ideal we had so earnestly pursued was coming apart and what began as a quiet ripple of discontent was ending in a tidal wave of rebellion.

As I became more aware of my responsibilities to the animals, I began to voice my opinions as to the management of the sheep, chiming in now and then about the placing of fences and other matters that the men considered their private domain. I was not so gently reminded that my best contribution could be made in the kitchen where I could do the 'things I was best at'. Since I was an equal partner, I had naturally assumed this meant an equal share in the decision-making as well, and I was less than pleased when I found I had to fight the good fight just to express my opinions, but lost the vote every time. Perhaps if I had donned a black singlet and gumboots, leaned over the fence and quoted how many sheep we ran to the acre and how much a bale of wool was worth, they'd have taken more notice. Since I was more concerned for the welfare of the sheep than the total numbers of the critters running on Aotea and had no idea what the wool was fetching, we faced a monumental communication gap.

I couldn't even excel at the so-called 'things I did best' and found I didn't fit the role of the dutiful farmer's wife who could feed a gang of shearers, teach five kids correspondence, help in the shed, provide a choice of delicacies for morning and afternoon teas and be content to be known to the Statistic Department as just plain 'farmer's wife'.

I refused to be relegated to the bed and breakfast brigade and since I was in the liberating mood, I issued Walt with an ultimatum — either I assumed what I considered my rightful place in the decision-making process, which for me meant a reaffirmation of our original purpose and a move away from the exploitation of the sheep, or I was leaving.

The farm had taken on a new meaning for the men. We were growing bigger, more conventional and the homesteading ideal was receding and taking with it the way of life we had travelled 16,000 kilometres to attain.

The annual mutilation of the lambs when they were castrated and tailed filled me with remorse and arguments over the ethics of such practices grew in intensity and number. Hardly a day went by without a bitter disagreement over what I saw as cruelty to the animals and a deliberate denial of my right to participate in the running of the farm. The battle reached its zenith one hot November day and I renounced my share of Aotea, lock, stock and wool bale.

With my entourage of dogs, cats, goats and pet sheep, I took off my wedding ring and became a liberated woman. I also became a vegetarian, giving up meat, fish and poultry, one small thing I could do for the animals to bring my actions into line with my professed concern for their welfare.

Many times I had blithely quoted 'To thine own self be true . . .' and, now that I had put my money where my mouth was, I discovered how achingly difficult it was to follow that adage. Suddenly there was nothing to life but an empty shell. I had my principles intact, but everything else was in tatters.

From 30 years of domestic activity that had spanned an ocean and pulsed with excitement and adventure, I stepped into a monastic-like solitude that for someone of my gregarious nature was almost unbearable. Informing the family in the States was a lesson in humility. It was an admission of defeat; the gallant cause I had espoused as they bade us bon voyage had failed. It was particularly difficult writing to my father, knowing how the thought of me alone somewhere on an island in the South Pacific would upset him.

In many ways, the 18 months I spent alone were the most difficult of my life, yet also the most enlightening. At first I sought refuge from the long, lonely hours and the frightening reality of my emancipation in glass after glass of homemade saki, enabling me to obliterate for a time the agony of being liberated. It took me some time to work through the grief and resentment and to come to understand just why the decision to leave Aotea had been so devastating. After all, wasn't I now free to do my own thing? Why then this terrible feeling of vulnerability and sadness instead of an exhilirating sense of emancipation? And this overwhelming sense of being alone – not lonely, for there is a difference – just alone.

In time, I came to realise that I had done myself a violence when I wrenched my roots from my homeland. Aotea had been a place where the severed tendrils, still tender and fragile, searching for permanency and a place of belonging, had reached out to take hold and root again. This desperate need was made more urgent when I became involved in the struggle for the wildlife. Aotea had then become a refuge, a shelter from the rude and hostile reactions that made trips to town a nightmare. Aotea was where my dreams and aspirations would come to fruition, a Utopia where we would live life as a part of the whole of creation and where I could thumb my nose at the opposition. I had created my own world, but it had been an illusion.

I understood what it meant to be a minority, an introduced species and this beautiful land of our choosing had become a prison. I had come searching for Paradise and had instead created my own hell from which there was no escape. I had no money and had renounced my U.S. citizenship in order to counter the oft-repeated attack that I was a foreigner trying to tell New Zealanders what to do with their wildlife. I had become a New Zealander, but it had made little difference to the attitude towards me. The world within and without had become hostile because of my belief that animals have rights and that our power over them demands compassion.

I had effectively estranged myself from the community and, because of the separation from Walt, many of our friends felt uneasy about visiting lest they appear to take sides. I had given up my share of Aotea and walked away from the homestead taking only personal belongings. I had shattered the thing I held most dear — my family.

For a long time, I agonised over giving up my convictions for the sake of unity and security, but knew it would be a sham, a pretence for appearances' sake. I would have repressed my true feelings and smouldered in resentment.

Many years have passed since I made my decision and while I regret the hurt it has caused, I know it was the only possible one for me. Many women are faced with an identity crisis, but most can do nothing about it. They have no place to run to. Many, because of their devotion to the family, refuse to put their own interests first. I was unable to be so gracious or selfless and stepped again into the unknown, only this time on a solo journey.

Though Walt was not far away, I seldom saw him and he

stubbornly refused to help me. He had taken my declaration of independence as a personal affront and retreated into his own world, just as I had retreated into mine. I was too proud to ask for assistance and therefore spent most of my time in exile searching for wood for the open fire and wood stove.

I would strongly recommend to my sisters that, should they decide to go it alone, they see to it that they are in a better position than I was. An island, perfect as it may be when getting away from it all, is not at all ideal when burning your bra and declaring your equality. First of all there is no-one around to appreciate your gestures of defiance and secondly, the complete absence of anyone to talk with and the non-existence of social outlets or activities to help fill the once busy hours can be devastating. Thirdly, hauling wood ad infinitum is hardly a satisfactory expression of liberation.

The bach in which I sought refuge belonged to a couple in Wellington who were undergoing their own middle-age crisis which ended in divorce, and as a result, the property was put up for sale. What little thought I had given to my future had included the hope that I could rent the bach, paying for it with the income derived from the sale of my writings and handicrafts. The prospect of the house being sold out from under me added to my anxieties.

I cursed my fate and began eyeing the henhouse with a view to renovating it for human occupation when, to my immense relief and surprise, I discovered that I had access to a small amount of capital that had been accumulated in the States for some years. Although the amount was modest and would in no way be adequate to purchase the house, it at least offered me a hope.

Another unexpected event brought me even closer to the point where I could make an offer for the bach. When I consulted a lawyer about turning over my share of Aotea, I found I was entitled to receive monetary compensation from Walt. These two unsolicited sources of revenue would make it possible for me to become a homeowner in the Sounds, complete with an acre of land and a mortgage.

The sense of relief at having a place of my own, a roof over my head, albeit a mortgaged one, gave me a new lease on life. At least now I could stay on the island if I chose to do so and thereby continue my fight for the wildlife.

The Arapawa orphans I had raised and to whom I was surrogate mother followed me dutifully to my new place of abode and took up residence under the house with a few assorted chickens. The space was adequate for my little band of refugees, but the height was such that sweeping out their droppings required that I either bend in half or crawl about on my hands and knees. My back would rebel at the unorthodox position and I'd attempt to stand erect and straighten my complaining spine, only to crack my head on the beams on so many occasions that I felt I'd wear a permanent dent in my skull.

The presence of the goats was a great comfort and their 'whither thou goest, I too will go' attitude touched me deeply. They had a comfortable sleeping arrangement at Aotea and need not have concerned themselves that I was no longer there; instead they had come to me in my time of need.

I often slept with them, appreciating the warmth of their bodies as they willingly shared their pallets of straw. We must have presented an unusual picture; one ageing expatriate, ex-wife, ex-everything, three little dogs tucked into the folds of my body and surrounded by 10 or 12 goats asleep in the hay under the house. The bach was even more exposed to southerly blasts, and the shakings and quakings through the long winter nights filled me with terror. Consequently I slept under the house more than I did inside it, gaining comfort from the nearness and warmth of the animals.

Somehow I made it through the winter and by the time spring arrived I was actually beginning to enjoy my freedom. I took long walks, something I had always savoured, but now I didn't have to concern myself about returning home at a given hour to prepare a meal or attend to some domestic chore. I could stay as long as I chose and there was much to keep me interested as enchanted hours sped by — listening, watching and learning. Often I returned as the sun was dipping behind the hills across the bay, and I slowly became aware that the prolonged excursions to the hills brought me a sense of peace, an emotion I had not experienced since I had left Aotea.

Usually the goats accompanied me on these outings and on several occasions I found myself at the head of a procession made up of the terriers (my constant companions), the tame Arapawa goats and 20-30 wild Arapawas that had seen us passing by and, curious, joined in to see where we were all going. They would follow us almost to the paddock by the house before sensing something was not quite right. They they would turn tail and, with a snort, rush back to their home in the hills. I'd often come across the wild pigs who still managed, with such encounters, to send a shiver down my spine, but since I respected and admired them and meant them no harm, they gave me safe passage through their territory and left me to my wanderings.

Though I had dreaded, in the first days of loneliness and melancholy, the rising of the sun and the prospect of yet another long, aimless day, life now began to assume a new significance and I found myself anticipating the dawn, wondering where the paths would take me that particular day, and what discoveries I would make. I was at peace with myself at last and found that I was humming, even smiling, as I went about the day to day business of living. I no longer felt afraid or lonely, vulnerable or guilty. In fact, although to some, the situation might not have seemed desirable, I was thoroughly enjoying myself. I had plenty of nothing and nothing was plenty for me. I had the sun in the morning and the moon at night, I could go to the hills when my heart was lonely. I had books, music, the sea on my doorstep providing a panorama of activity; I had the animals for whom all this had come to pass, and of late, I had found a new interest. It was during my self-imposed exile that I began to make a record of events that had occurred since that fateful night I had shouted above the noise of the traffic: 'Let's chuck it, Walt'.

How long ago that seemed. Things had not gone quite as I had anticipated and, had we known what lay ahead, I wondered if we would have left. Most of life is unpredictable, and fortunately so, or our world would have remained a very static place indeed.

Although my dreams of what might have been still brought tears to my eyes, I felt a certain satisfaction in what my toss of the cards had brought. I had come, albeit the hard way, to a better understanding of myself and had not betrayed those principles I held most dear. I had seen the children to maturity, marriage and parenthood. We had taken them as far as we could; now they must make their own way. I had fought for the animals and, although victory was not ours and many of the animals lay dead, I knew I had done my best and was not numbered amongst those that caused their demise. I had met many wonderful people as a result of the involvement with the wildlife and had made dear and trusted friends whose love and support sustained me. On balance, I had to admit that the animals had done more for me than I ever did for them. They brought me an awareness and an awakening, the joy of true and lasting friendships, the opportunity to test my inner strength and find I was not wanting. All in all it hadn't been such a 'bad go', but how I wished I could have shared the sweet taste of satisfaction with Walt, and that our goals and aspirations had found a mutual garden in which to flourish.

I walked this day, as I did each day, to the beach in search of wood. The goats strolled along nibbling seaweed and other delicacies, stopping now and then to clash horns or chase one another around my legs. Some of my 'ladies' were getting a bit matronly for this sort of sprightly behaviour and I watched with amusement as Samantha, now in her eighth year, disciplined her latest set of twins. My dear friend Jody had died not long before. Cradled in my arms, she drew her last feeble breath as I rocked her, sobbing words of endearment. We had buried that gentle, trusting friend in the garden at Aotea. Now her two daughters, placid and timid like Jody, walked with me.

As we came to the mouth of the creek, my attention was attracted by a shag with a large fish clasped firmly in her bill and heading for the sea. It occurred to me how much the cats would appreciate a change of diet and since the fish appeared dead, but still fresh and of a good size, I issued the challenge.

'Okay, Madam Shag, I'll have that fish!' And I set off in hot pursuit. What I thought would be an easy conquest became a marathon of wit and will. Up and down the beach we raced. I assume she must have been as middle-aged as I, for she was heaving and puffing on a par with my own gaspings, but she would not for one moment relinquish her hold on the fish. I blocked her escape when she made advances towards the sea and she seemed incapable of taking to the wing with her burden and thereby eluding me. She spread her wings when she ran to give added momentum and balance and looked at once both comical and defiant.

Sam rolled her eyes to indicate all this racing about was most undignified and stalked off down the beach, removing her offspring from the spectacle of a tiny shag named David being pursued by a greying Goliath. After some 30 minutes of dodging, darting and eyeballing one another, I conceded defeat. With a laugh and a sweeping bow to show my admiration for the little creature's tenacity, I backed away. Stepping deliberately, with head held high, she waddled slowly and regally into the sea. There she turned a baleful eye in my direction and with a victorious toss of her head, paddled off to her home amongst the rocks. The cats also cast a baleful eye as they ate their monotonous fare of egg and milk. I suggested they do their own fishing from now on.

In the summertime, the goats would often come up on the verandah of the bach to sleep and frequently the dogs and I would join them there, sleeping under the millions of stars that pierce the night skies of the Sounds. It was there I discovered that the nights are full of activity and conversations, and as I fell asleep to the familiar rhythm of the goats chewing their cuds and the hoot of the morepork, I would become aware of the grumblings of the wild pigs, the sniffling of the hedgehogs and feel, rather than hear, the flight of the bats.

Other sounds penetrated the night — whistles, screeches and the bumptious gatherings of the geese who seemed to meet during the darkest hours. Whatever they discussed at night, they discussed it at length and I gathered it was of some importance to the flock since they all participated and all had much to say. Unfortunately, this nightly gathering was most often held under my bedroom window and could be easily overheard from the verandah. Thus many of the other sounds I should have liked to distinguish were lost in all the goose grumblings.

I had succeeded in making a life for myself that had brought a measure of happiness and contentment, and was not prepared when Walt began to intrude once again into my daily routine, bringing to the surface emotions I considered I had put to rest. On my 52nd birthday, I responded to a tap on the door and looked up from my typing to see Walt standing on the verandah with a bouquet of flowers and a gift he had made for the occasion. I was shocked, surprised and for one of the few times in my life, quite speechless!

Walt and I had had a minimum of contact during our estrangement, except when we joined forces to bury Jody or to meet the needs of the children. We had made a pact that nothing would interfere with our responsibilities as parents and in no way would we put the children in a position where they would have to choose between us. Our differences were ours, not theirs, and we did all we could to shield them.

Now Walt had come the 500 metres which required few steps, but an enormous amount of humility and I felt deeply touched by his gesture. The spontaneous side of my nature wanted to run to him, throw my arms around his neck and assure him everything would be all right, but I could not will myself to move. Something held me back and I could only hesitantly accept the gift and flowers, politely thank him and lapse into an awkward silence as deep and prolonged as his own.

I realised as I sat watching him across the table that I no longer held any resentment. The hurt and frustration at his inability to understand my position had receded. We each had to do what we thought was right and, for one of Walt's rather conventional upbringing, my rebellion had been a tremendous blow to his masculine

173

pride. I knew he suffered from the separation just as I had and I grieved to have caused him pain, for we had had 30 years together, a sharing not easily cast aside.

As the days passed, Walt became a frequent visitor to the bach and eventually, a permanent one.

I blame it all on Roger Whitaker who was displaying his considerable talent singing that lovely melody *Feelings* as I sat across the room from Walt at Aotea. Debbie and Mitch now lived at the homestead and had invited me over for the evening. Walt, of course, was there and as Roger crooned on, Walt rose from his chair and, bowing deeply, asked: 'May I have this dance?'

For an estranged couple, we were holding each other very close indeed and I found my own feelings spinning completely out of control. All the hard-earned reserve fostered during my time alone melted and I longed for Walt's love and companionship, for conversation and human interaction.

Walt and I spent our second honeymoon in the boatshed, for Roy, Marc and their children had arrived and we vacated the bach for them. They now had a baby daughter, Kirstie, making them a sizeable family of six and, since Walt and I were feeling intimate, a one-room boatshed was more appropriate than a three-bedroom house for talking, touching and renewing our love. However, before we could break out the orange blossom and champagne, we had to evict several families of kiore, who had built the most exquisite nests from bits of bone and scraps of wool.

Roy and Marc stayed a few weeks and it was during this visit that they expressed their desire to move to the island permanently. Obviously, should this ever come to pass, the bach with its numerous rooms, was the only suitable accommodation for them and since it was illegal to live in the boatshed, Walt and I, should we decide to remain together, would have to make other arrangements. We could combine our talents under one roof or look into his and hers lodgings somewhere on Aotea.

At about this time, Debbie and Mitch decided to purchase the farm property adjoining Aotea, a decision that would make the financial situation very difficult for many years to come, and exacerbate the problems between Walt and me by adding to his responsibilities and involving us more deeply in sheep farming.

There was one very good reason for me to encourage the purchase; it meant yet another safe area for the wildlife and, since the government refused to assist us or grant the animals any sort of protection from poachers, hunter and the Forest Service, it fell to us to provide what safety and security we could. I felt torn between the desire to provide further sanctuary for the animals and the fear that the acquisition of more land would only add to the difficulties within our relationship, so recently restored and at best uncertain. There never seemed to be any gain for the animals that did not involve some sort of sacrifice.

Otanerau, as the new farm was known, had, tucked away amongst the trees, what was left of the original homestead. It was behind this relic that the volunteers had pitched their tents on the three occasions they had come to rescue the goats. Nestled between ancient stone walls and a noisy, chattering creek, the old building had about it an aura of charm and potential beauty. I had always loved the place and felt the neglect of decades could be reversed by a bit of tender, loving care. Walt agreed.

Walt and I agreed to co-exist in the heap of rubble so as to make Roy's venture to the island a possibility and once again we became gypsies. We moved our few belongings into a hastily erected shed and with the help of our dear friend, Ken, a carpenter by trade, managed to make one room of the homestead habitable before the first boatload of Roy's and Marc's furniture arrived. By the third boatload, the bach was bulging at the seams and I wondered if order could ever be made of the chaos. Roy, Marc, four children, three cats and one huge black dog named Mika were ferried ashore from the yacht with the last load of their belongings. They were to stay for two years before financial difficulties forced them to return to the mainland.

During those two years, Walt and I fought our cold war while moulding the homestead into a cosy and comfortable home. My goats, ever faithful, followed me to yet another hideaway and, much to Walt's dismay, took up residence on the new back porch he had built. They settled in with such alacrity, I believe they thought he had spent all that time and energy just for their convenience. They staged a 'lie-in' every night and since we had to traverse the porch to get to the bathroom, the trip to answer nature's call became a feat of dexterity, stepping between, over and around the reclining bodies of a dozen or more goats. Should Walt be foolish enough to try it without the benefit of a light, the outcome was a predictable shuffling and stomping about as the goats were disturbed, followed by curses and bad-tempered threats as he stumbled his way to the bathroom door.

Living under one roof, leaks and all, required a considerable amount of restraint on both of our parts and in many ways the forced confinement proved therapeutic. Of itself, it provided a lesson in survival as we hauled water from the creek, tried to keep what was left of the homestead from blowing away in the southerlies, froze in the winter and tried, humanely, to remove several thousand bees from the eves under the roof.

Just how to go about evicting the little honey makers who were definitely in no mood to cooperate, we were not quite sure. We had been advised by all and sundry that we would have to burn them out or kill them with spray. I refused to accept those methods and for a time we sought to ignore them. They in turn, however, would not ignore us and hovered uncomfortably close as we laboured on the house. Our decision to remove them came after they caught Walt and I painting the roof with hot tar. We had built a fire in a circle of rocks and when the wind shifted, blowing the smoke through the abode of the bees, they emerged feeling anything but friendly and honed in on us, buzzing menacingly. By the time we had done our cat-on-a-hot-tarred-roof act, falling over one another in our haste to get down the ladder, we resembled two tar babies. Now Walt, looking like an invader from outer space in his anti-sting outfit, approached the wary bees singing *Puff, the Magic Dragon* as he released small amounts of smoke in their direction from the smouldering can he held in his well-gloved hand.

I don't know if it was his singing or one Magic Dragon puff too many, but the bees were neither impressed nor subdued and began swarming angrily around him. One perturbed little fellow managed to wriggle inside the netting covering Walt's head and neck, and his eyes crossed and rolled as he tried to focus on the intruder buzzing ominously about his face. Fortunately, the bee flew out from under the veil, perhaps by the same route he had entered, and to Walt's immense relief, caused no harm.

However, Walt was now surrounded by literally thousands of bees humming and buzzing in a most unfriendly manner and I begged him to abandon the idea and escape, but he stood his ground. He said later that he had the impression the bees were only trying to frighten him and did not mean to attack, which was why he proceeded to place layer upon layer of their honeycombs in boxes and calmly climb down the ladder, walk some distance from the house and relocate the nest in the trees. Most of the bees followed, leaving only a few bewildered stragglers flying about wondering what had happened.

The bees accepted the transplanting of their colony and reformed their hive about the boxes. All Walt received was a sting on the back of his hand. It took tremendous courage to stay on that roof once the bees began displaying their opposition, real or feigned, but he managed, with an outwardly calm and deliberate approach, to complete the operation successfully and humanely.

I maintained my financial independence and we shared the chores rather than dividing them into the conventional his and hers categories. Neither of us altered our stand on the issues that had led to our separation and I remained as articulate in defence of my hard-won freedoms and convictions, as ever. It was at times an uneasy truce and we lived in a state of armed readiness should disagreements flare, which they frequently did.

Since both Aotea and the bach were occupied and we had no place left to go to get away from the conflict and confrontations, we were forced to communicate, face our problems, admit differences and find solutions. We are still seeking solutions and perhaps always will, but our forced confinement has made dialogue necessary and there is a great healing in bridging the communication gap.

Marc and the children adjusted to life at Aotea with remarkable ease, and soon Marc was prowling the hills enjoying an intimacy with the island that only a few have known. Hardly a day went by without seeing her pass either on her way to or coming from her walks of discovery. She cooked for her army on a miniature wood stove, taught the three eldest children and became to me the best of friends.

Debbie, meanwhile, was making her nest at Aotea homestead. She and Mitch had two children, leaving her little spare time for 'prowling' and indeed, the great walkabouts that Marc so enjoyed did not appeal to Debbie. She became the beachcomber, searching for, finding and recording the numerous artifacts that attested to Maori occupation in the long ago. She and Little Bertha got along splendidly and accomplished the most remarkable things together. Little Bertha looked a bit smug with all Debbie's beautiful culinary creations sitting on her shelf — I had never been able to achieve with Bertha that which Debbie managed so easily. Bertha gave me the distinct impression that the deficiency had been mine, for look what she could do with a competent partner! She now sported a hood of copper and had been painted black to fit in with the remodelling of the kitchen. Debbie had laid a hearth of stone at Bertha's feet and she did look very respectable indeed.

Debbie had been a friend before she married Mitch and now with

Marc, we three shared a wonderful togetherness, a love of the island and the enjoyment of many of the same activities. We had become almost a community and the extended family situation was both novel and challenging. We were able to assist one another with the children and share our individual talents. Both young mothers were creative, intelligent, capable and continually amazed me with their versatility and accomplishments.

Marc's house was usually bursting with activity. Four children, plus one or two others Marc often had visiting, kept things humming. There always seemed to be cause for celebration and whether the gatherings were spontaneous eruptions or planned occasions such as birthdays or Christmas, they were full of joy and noisy confusion. It was madcap and fun. It was family.

Mary, Mark and their two children would come to be with us when Mark's work allowed and I could but marvel at this complex and diverse gathering of individuals that had become the Rowe family.

It was while Roy and Marc were living on the island that Craig Ferguson, a friend and member of the New Zealand Deerstalkers' Association, organised a fourth muster of the island's wildlife to try to save the few wild remnants of the goat population from a further assault by the Forest Service.

David Lange's Labour Government had swept to power with a snap election and I heaved a great sigh of relief, believing that the fate of the animals would at last change for the better. I was bitterly disappointed to find that the new Minister of Lands and Forests was taking the same course as his National Party predecessors and was accepting the same biased advice without the benefit of the consultations the election had promised. Protestations that governments are not run by public servants, but by well-informed Ministers with a full grasp of their portfolios cannot, in my experience, be sustained. The Ministers I have dealt with all seem to me to have been led around by the nose, with the tail wagging the dog, not the dog, the tail.

We approached the new Minister immediately after the election to request a re-evaluation of the situation and an opportunity to present our case in the new atmosphere of Labour's catchphrase 'one for all, and all for one'.

Labour people had tried to assist us when they were in opposition and had openly agreed with my efforts on behalf of the animals. I assumed it would be a simple matter for them to translate their professed support into a totally new approach to the island's wildlife and, for the first time, the animals would get a fair hearing. Alas and alack, there was no evidence that an election had actually taken place insofar as the new government's attitude was concerned. The tone and the content of the correspondence had changed in only two ways — the first, that there was a new signature and secondly, by the addition of the salutory phrase 'Kia ora'.

When we became aware that the Forest Service was planning another assault against the wildlife, we endeavoured, by numerous phone calls to various Ministers' offices, by letters and by telegrams, all at considerable expense, to thwart the planned action and establish a dialogue to seek a positive solution rather than the 'if it moves, shoot it!' mentality of the last three National governments. We wanted an opportunity to present the facts to those who had professed to support and agree with us on the preservation of the wildlife, but no amount of pleading by Craig, Celia, Ashley or me could change the course of events.

Craig rang me to say that he had inquired as to the level of interest amongst some of his fellow deerstalkers in an attempt to remove the few remaining goats from the reserve before the Forest Service arrived. Some 30 members said they would come to the island at their own expense. This would be our final bid to save the Arapawa wildlife.

CHAPTER XIV

Follow the Heart

The Knowledgables had deemed it a compromise to erect a fence around the central portion of the reserve, thereby isolating the most sensitive vegetation from both wild and domestic animals. The idea of a fence had been suggested many times over the years, but each time it had been dismissed by the Knowledgables as inappropriate.

Now, however, with the costs having escalated to several times what they would have been had the original idea been acted upon, and with most of the animals the fence was meant to exclude now either dead or removed, the government, at the eleventh hour, saw fit to surround the vegetation with a solar-powered electric fence.

Before Craig and the deerstalkers could plan their muster, it was necessary for a portion of the fence, as yet uncompleted, to be closed off. This was the responsibility of the Park Board. It seemed fairly straightforward; we needed to know the fence would be secure before we brought the animals out since they must not be permitted to return to within its confines.

The government department responsible did not give us the needed assurances until a mere fortnight before the muster was to commence. We worked with a sense of urgency as the Forest Service was chomping at the bit to get to the island. Craig, Ashley and I spent weeks writing letters, telephoning and sending telegrams in an effort to sort things out and, although assurances were eventually given, in reality they were not acted upon. When Craig and the 30 deerstalkers, Ashley, Yvonne, Marc and others of the family completed the day-long muster, they found the fence still incomplete.

When I questioned this, I was told that the weather had not been suitable. However, as we knew full well what the weather conditions had been prior to the muster, we could not accept this explanation. To me, it was just another in a long line of stumbling blocks used by the government departments intent upon pursuing inflexible policies.

The next turn of the screw came when we were informed that the goats would not be permitted to inhabit the southern portion of the unfenced reserve. A part of the compromise made on behalf of the animals was that they should have freedom from the systematic shooting that now prevailed, so long as they remained outside the fenced area. Now this partial protection was being withdrawn and I bristled with resentment.

Suddenly the weather, considered by the authorities as too bad to allow the workers to come to the island to complete the fence as promised, now seemed quite acceptable and, within days after the deerstalkers had returned to the mainland, the fence was completed and the animals remaining within were trapped.

The Forest Service moved in with the rapidity I had expected and claimed to have shot 114 goats. This was strange, indeed, since the 30 volunteers had seen only 15 goats when they combed the reserve from the axial ridge to the shores of Cook Strait.

The wild sheep remaining within the fenced area were exempt from the shooting, we were assured. They were to be uplifted by helicopter and set free outside the fence. That this was an extremely expensive and dangerous operation bothered the authorities not at all. It was only taxpayers' money. There was not so much as a wink for the goats, despite my protestations of favouritism and duplicity. The pigs were never spared a thought.

The final blow came when it was discovered that the fence was not operating effectively and the remedy suggested was to cover the existing fence with netting. I immediately objected on humanitarian grounds as the netting was a potential death trap for the animals who could easily become entangled with their horns. Should this occur, I pointed out, the goats could languish for many weeks and months before anyone might wander into the remote reserve. This could mean a slow, lingering death. This possibility was brought to the attention of the authorities by telephone and letter. In their reply, they said: '. . . and while we accept that there is some potential for goats to get caught in the upper and wider gaps in the wire, there is no opportunity to change plans'.

The work was begun and a further nail in the coffin of an endangered species was hammered into place. A ray of enlightenment was beginning to shimmer on the horizon, however. The Director of the Wildlife Service had stated publicly that the goats should be protected and three Cabinet Ministers declared the goats met the international criteria for an endangered species. Another positive step was a change in the chairmanship of the Park Board.

Goats, particularly those with cashmere potential, were now being mooted as a possible economic salvation for the country's financial difficulties. This did not assist the Arapawa goats as they now became the targets for live poaching, to be sold to the highest bidder, but at least it did point up the total absurdity of the government's policies. They had wantonly and knowingly slaughtered a national resource worth millions of dollars and used the taxpayers' money to do it all.

In his book, *Never Cry Wolf*, Farley Mowat writes: 'Whenever and wherever men have engaged in the mindless slaughter of animals (including other men), they have often attempted to justify their acts by attributing the most vicious or revolting qualities to those they would destroy; and the less reason there is for the slaughter, the greater the campaign of vilification'.

Thus it has been for the wildlife of Arapawa. For twelve years, we have pitted our wit and will against a mindless bureaucracy. I have seen a good many of those in authority come and go, sweeping into office like a chill wind. I have heard the thunder, the threats, the cajoling, the deceit, and wonder indeed how we are governed at all. Bureaucracy is a play acted out by bureaucrats and when I entered their halls I found all the actors in place; the heavies, the comedians, heroes and heroines, sincere and honest troubadours, villains and bastards.

The curtain opened on this saga which has claimed twelve years of my life, upon a woman hesitant, yet hopeful; a woman who knew nothing of the battle that lay ahead. I was dreaming my impossible dreams and reaching for unreachable stars. I believed this land of milk and honey to which we'd come would satisfy our greatest expectations.

Suddenly there were the animals crying out and I could not walk away. Instead I walked deeper into the tunnel. As the months ticked by into years, I lurched from one bureaucratic blunder and insult to another, and whether the abuse was directed at me personally or towards the animals, I somehow picked up the pieces and slowly grew in determination and awareness.

I came to know what it is to be hated, scorned, mocked and insulted, an alien among aliens. I knew the fear and self-loathing of the coward as I ground my way to rock bottom. Gradually the inner gel turned to an iron rod and hesitancy became conviction.

Along the way I have seen humankind at its lowest and most cruel, and I also saw it elevated to the highest levels of love and compassion.

I have been privileged to know the great beauty, mystery and savage rage of the island; to have shared my bed with her wild creatures. There has been laughter and love aplenty; uplifting love of the richest kind, and sorrow deeper than the oceans at my door.

Why has this island claimed my heart, and for what reason did the unfortunate wildlife invade my conscience? Why the compelling need to remain despite the emotional and physical difficulties? There are places more alluring, yet the intensity of the island's raw beauty fills me with humility and awe. It has about it a timeless, undisturbed aura; an oldness, a permanence.

Deep within the forest I can hear the rumble and indignant quarrels of the pigs. The wild sheep, brown and ancient, watch with soft dark eyes, wise and knowing. The goats, timid and wary, monuments to a bygone era, call softly to me and know I am their friend.

I sit and watch the barren, rugged hills shine with a fire of gold as the sun reflects on the clay and baked earth. It succeeds in making lovely that which, of itself, is unlovely; for the beauty of the island is the patchwork of earth, sky and sea, a life force blown through it by the ever-present wind.

The island has convulsed itself through the ages and thrust upward into jagged peaks and deep gullies, carpeted with fern and stinging nettle. Its placid creeks and streams can become gorged and raging torrents within minutes as the heavens open and the enraged gods seek to obliterate all in a purge of water. As the skies clear, the island becomes an emerald, the various shades of green sparkling and shimmering in the sun. Rainbows, arcs of vibrating colour, stretch from valley to hilltop across the bay.

The wedgewood blue of the sea is emblazoned with a million sparkling diamonds that dance like elves on each droplet of water, or on an angry day, the water gathers itself into a funnel of grey fury and, whipped by the madness of the wind, spirals across the bay screaming and demented, hurling itself at the hills. Clouds race across the sky; Valkyries thundering to Valhalla, creating a mosaic of shadow and light.

Gulls, plovers, oyster catchers screech and whistle as they vie with shags, herons and paradise ducks for the delicacies along the shore. The curious fantail, my little messenger of hope, flits around minding everybody's business. At night I trip over a pair of hedgehogs shuffling around in the dark and, as I apologise, I see a huge, powerful shadow moving just outside the ring of lantern light and smell the strong scent of the wild pig. He growls, not unlike a bear, and I freeze in my tracks, frightened, yet thrilled to be so close to this elusive and feared creature of the forest. I see the shadow race past and disappear into the blackness and make my way to the house, wondering if he watches.

I heave a sigh of relief when I step on to the back porch.

The goats are there and I stop to speak with them and bid them good night. How beautiful they are and how I despair of the suffering they have endured. The Knowledgables are now blaming the demise of the rare snails on the goats as well as the pigs. Despite their insistence that the goats must be shot to preserve the vegetation, they now say that the vegetation is not regenerating after all. We can only account for 60 of the goats; the others are either shot or captured by poachers. The once vibrant, beautiful herd is reduced to a handful of survivors.

The wild sheep have fared better, although they too are subjected to poaching. At least they have a protected status and are now thought of as other than vermin. The wily pig may outrun and outbreed his hunters. I pray that this is so.

I sit and shake my head, recalling the zany, the tragic, the hilarious, and marvel that I have shared in so much. How dull life in Pennsylvania seemed by comparison.

I say to myself, 'Be still my heart, let go, walk away and find peace', but I know I cannot. Wherever I go or life may take me, part of me will always be here. I have cried me a river and loved me an island. Somewhere I found the courage to fight for the wildlife, now I must find the strength to accept defeat, and hope that from the experiences and knowledge gained, other wildlife in New Zealand will stand a better chance.

I do not believe it has been in vain as some will say. True, the wildlife of Arapawa is now fragmented and dispersed, but from it all has come an awareness and a caring. Perhaps it is this caring that will prevent the goats from becoming extinct. We have brought them this far, others must now join and continue the struggle on their behalf. It would be impossible for me to list all the names of those who have contributed to this call of the wild, but may I say thank you from the bottom of my heart. You are the Beautiful People.

Epilogue

I began to look to the future with growing apprehension. I was not yet beyond caring for the animals in a practical sense, but one day I would be. There was also the possibility that Aotea would, at some future date, change hands and the animals could then be unwelcome guests.

Plantings of pine trees in the bay and the fenced reserve area has further restricted the movements of the animals and the government has pursued its policy of no-policy and benign neglect, giving no indication of interest or assistance.

The thoughts of who would care for the animals if I were to become ill or die became an obsession, obliterating all else. Then, over the Christmas holidays, we received a visit from some lovely people who had heard about the goats and, while cruising in the Sounds, had decided to come and see them and hear the story for themselves. They were among many who had called in over the years and I was grateful as always, for the interest and concern. Our visitors spent the day and as they prepared to leave, I asked for their address. I had felt particularly drawn to the woman in the group and while, at the time, there seemed no reason to further the acquaintance, I still felt strongly compelled to know where they could be contacted.

In the ensuing months, I floundered and faltered as I searched for workable, practical solutions to the problem of securing a future for the wildlife. One thought had been to leave the island, taking as many of the animals with me as possible, but the staggering cost of suitable land soon made that a prohibitive choice. In any case, leaving the island was not an alternative I wished to contemplate, not only because of my personal attachment to it, but because of the strong conviction that the wildlife belong here.

While no good, kind fairy waved a wand and sorted out all my frustrations and anxieties, a few bits of fairy dust must have floated down to this mere mortal, for suddenly the clouds of indecision began to lift.

My house of the 500 Metre Revolt would be the vehicle that would turn 300 acres of Aotea into a lovely, shimmering refuge — a sanctuary in perpetuity. The revenue from the sale of the house would enable me to secure the area.

An enormous amount of work was required to bring the house up to a standard that would attract the amount of money I estimated for fences, shed, accommodation, etc and once again Walt turned his numerous skills to the renovating process.

The following year was a blur of sanding, painting and papering with a bit of fencing thrown in for good measure. When the time finally arrived to place the property on the market, I contacted a land agent, wrote to friends for the names of possible potential buyers and, acting on impulse, sent a resume about the bach to the visitors of that sunny, summer day.

Out of the blue they had sailed and many months had passed since they had come to Aotea, yet something within me directed me to contact them. Soon Margaret, the woman I had felt drawn to, was on the phone telling me she was interested in the bach and within months she and a friend had made the purchase.

Was it just a coincidence they came to Arapawa? Now there is the money for the fences, a jetty, sheds and a small cabin for me, enabling me to remain near to the wildlife . . . at least for a while yet. Long enough to create a place of peace and safety, a place that says 'I'm sorry for man's folly and lack of compassion', a place for the animals to live out their lives in a social structure of their choosing with a minimum of interference.

It will not be for our children's children, nor for the benefit of the human species, but for the animals themselves that they may live with dignity without having to justify their right to life by benefiting mankind in some way.

Their survival will be for their own enrichment, their possible economic potential *deliberately overlooked*. Their gene-pool will be for *their* progeny, not ours. The Arapawa Sanctuary will be our gift of love to the animals, and perhaps one day, they will look down from their mountain refuge and understand that we make this gesture to bridge the chasm, the climb down from the pinnacle upon which we have placed ourselves and to accept our place amongst them.

I once said to myself:

'*Be still my heart*'. And now it beats faster with the anticipation of a new beginning.

'*Let go and walk away*'. I feel the need of the Arapawa wildlife and know I never could.

'*Find peace*'. I have.